Grow A Pair

Jim Burgen
and
Scott Nickell

Edited by Ben Foote

Grow A Pair
Published by Jim Burgen and Scott Nickell
© 2011 by Jim Burgen and Scott Nickell

First Paperback Edition

Cover design by Josh Maynard
Edited by Ben Foote

ALL RIGHTS RESERVED
No portion of this book may be reproduced, stored in a retrieval system, or transmitted in any form or by any means – electronic, mechanical, photocopy, recording, or other – except for brief quotations in printed reviews, without the prior permission of the publisher.

All scripture quotations, unless otherwise indicated, are taken from the HOLY BIBLE, NEW INTERNATIONAL VERSION®, NIV®. Copyright© 1973, 1978, 1984 by International Bible Society. Used by permission of Zondervan, www.zondervan.com. All rights reserved.

Scripture quotations noted **ESV** are taken from the HOLY BIBLE, ENGLISH STANDARD VERSION®, ESV®. Copyright© 2001 by Crossway, a publishing ministry of Good News Publishers. Used by permission. All rights reserved.

ISBN: 978-0-9835618-5-9

Printed by Centennial Printing in Louisville, Colorado

This title is also available as an eBook: ISBN 978-0-9835618-4-2

For information:
Flatirons Community Church
355 W South Boulder Road
Lafayette, Colorado 80026

www.flatironschurch.com

Table of Contents

Introduction 01

01. Grow A Pair... Of What? 03
[General Discussion Questions] 20
[Discussion Questions for Women] 22

02. Joseph and Chuck... Identity and Integrity 25
[General Discussion Questions] 46
[Discussion Questions for Women] 48

03. Samson and Vinnie... Strength and Wisdom 51
[General Discussion Questions] 77
[Discussion Questions for Women] 79

04. David, Part One... Humility 81
[General Discussion Questions] 98
[Discussion Questions for Women] 100

05. David, Part Two... Learning From Mistakes 103
[General Discussion Questions] 122
[Discussion Questions for Women] 124

06. Boaz... Honor and Protectiveness 127
[General Discussion Questions] 149
[Discussion Questions for Women] 151

Epilogue 153
Appendix 159
About the Authors 165

Introduction
A note from Jim Burgen and Scott Nickell

The book you now hold in your hands is the written form of a series of messages that we delivered during the weekend services at Flatirons Community Church located in Lafayette, Colorado. While some editing was necessary to convert the spoken word to written form, we have attempted to maintain the same rhythm, tone, and integrity that one would find if listening to the messages at church.

Grow A Pair addresses biblical manhood. However, at the core, the teachings found in this book are not limited to men. Instead, this book simply uses male examples found in the Bible to highlight characteristics that everybody – men and women – should hold dear in their lives: *identity*, *integrity*, *strength*, *wisdom*, *humility*, *a willingness to learn from mistakes*, *honor*, and *protectiveness*.

Since *Grow A Pair* solely uses male examples to demonstrate the importance of these characteristics, we've included individual sets of questions specifically designed for women after every chapter. We hope that these discussion questions will spark conversations as well as illuminate the need for these characteristics in the lives of women.

Whether you choose to sit in a church building and listen to a live teacher, listen online, read words displayed on an electronic screen, or read words printed on a sheet of paper… the goal is always the same: that you would have the chance to consider what Jesus defines as *truth*. He promises that if we are willing to hold on to this *truth*, then he will use it to set us free… free from the same, old results and outcomes that have defined our lives in the past… and free to experience the better life that God offers.

We sincerely hope that this book relays Jesus' *truth* in an easily understandable and relatable manner, and we sincerely hope that you consider adjusting to his *truth* – it will make a world of difference in your life.

01.
Grow A Pair... Of What?

By
Jim Burgen

01.
Grow A Pair... Of What?

Grow A Pair.

Awesome.

Very few pastors can get away with naming their book *Grow A Pair*. Somehow, Scott and I pulled it off. I can't imagine some of my former pastors and teachers trying to approach this subject in their churches: *Brothers and sisters... today, I would like to talk to you about what it means to 'grow a pair'.* There would be riots! There would be families storming out the door and old women crying!

Yet here you are, holding the book in your hands, curiously reading the first chapter. I'm really glad.

I understand that, when you buy a book about Jesus with a title as provocative as ours, you are entitled to an explanation. That is exactly what this first chapter is about. This chapter is simply an introduction. In fact, the only application you will find in this chapter goes like this: *Will you please consider reading the rest of this book?*

Some of you might not be familiar with the phrase, "Grow a pair." First of all, welcome to Earth. Second, let me explain it to you. "Grow a pair," is a phrase that you direct toward a man (surprise!) who isn't acting in what you consider to be a manly fashion. Most of the time, men are the ones hurling this phrase at other men. I like to believe that, although the phrase obviously carries a tinge of insult, it *mostly* offers encouragement! This is a shallow and shaky justification, I know. Oh well...

The phrase, "Grow a pair," implies that a man isn't acting like he should because he has lost contact with a couple of precious items that God gave him (for those of you who are still confused, you should probably have a close friend or family member explain the 'anatomy' of this phrase before you're totally lost). In the end, the phrase suggests that if said man could locate, replace, or 'grow' said lost items, then maybe he could 'man up' and begin acting like the person he was created to be.

In a way, this is the theory that unpacks itself throughout the rest of this book.

Why grow a pair?

I have several reasons for wanting to write *Grow A Pair*, and I want you to understand these reasons because you might be tempted to put this book down. You might have convinced yourself that you know where this material is headed. You might be tempted to throw it away before considering its teachings. So... just stick around for, at least, one chapter.

One reason I want to write this book is because, in my opinion, the definition of manhood has been diluted by current American culture. According to my observation of American culture over the last several years, our definition of manhood has been watered down and neutered by the idea that 'we are all the same'.

I believe the castration of the American male actually began with a noble fight for equality between genders. I use the word 'noble' because I genuinely mean it. I believe in equality. Jesus believed in equality. However, somewhere down the line, we began confusing 'equality' with 'sameness', and this is dangerous. Men and women are *not* the same. We are absolutely equal in value and worth, but we are simply not the same. [1]

The truth is, for countless years, women have been unjustly treated as second-class human beings, and a noble fight for equality spawned from this mistreatment, but the answer for equality is not to tear men down. Instead, the answer is to build women up.

I also believe that nowhere else on the planet, at least in recent years, have men bought into the idea of surrendering their manhood more than in the church. At some point in history, people started teaching that men must surrender their hopes, dreams, personalities, and masculinity in order to become followers of Jesus Christ. Therefore, people began believing that Christian men must become wimpy, starry-eyed, asexual, spineless, and passive. Let's be honest, many of us were raised to believe that Jesus himself was a quiet and weak victim of bullies. While usually unspoken, the understood message to men from many churches can be summed up like this: *If you want to follow Jesus, please surrender your spine, personality, testicles, and thus, your manhood… and only then will Jesus be able to use you.*

Therefore, one of the reasons I want to teach about biblical manhood is because I want to clarify God's *actual* definition of manhood. If I were a man (which… I am) and the Bible taught to surrender my manhood (which… it doesn't), then I would never even consider following Jesus.

The other reason I want to write a book about the concept of 'growing a pair' stands in stark contrast to that of emasculation. I've observed that many men in our culture believe that, simply because they were born males, they have a God-given right to bully, intimidate, demand, and dominate: *I can do whatever I want because 'I'm the man'. I'm stronger and more powerful. I'm richer and have a bigger... truck.*

Oftentimes, masculinity is not measured by a man's character, but by how many women he has conquered, diminished, and dumped. Sometimes, manhood is measured by a man's ability to fertilize a woman rather than his ability to father or parent a child. As a matter of fact, half of a generation is currently being raised with the concept of a father as a mere sperm donor. They observe nothing more from their own fathers, and they expect nothing more of themselves.

I wish I could say that this behavior was limited to those who live outside the church, but that would be a lie. Many times, the church has promoted the same destructive view of manhood. Pastors will misquote Jesus and say, *Men are supposed to be the bosses of their homes. Wives, girlfriends, and children are simply employees of the man, and they must unquestionably jump when the man says 'jump' because... it's in the Bible.*

For the record, those concepts are *not* in the Bible. Those types of pastors use distorted terms like 'boss' and 'master', when the Bible uses terms like 'leader' and 'head'. In fact, anytime an author of the Bible tells men to be leaders of their homes, that same author immediately points to Jesus as the prime example of leadership. Nowhere in the Bible do you find Jesus sitting in a recliner, telling people to pick up his socks and shoes, cook his dinner, and keep the kids out of his hair because 'he's the man'.

Whether we've bought into the concept of emasculation or the concept of domination, the truth is that most men are living their lives by an incredibly distorted definition of manhood. Honestly, many men (maybe *most* men) aren't being very good leaders. Either we don't know how to be good leaders, or we're too scared to try anything new.

Can a lady grow a pair?

Before you continue reading, I want to make one thing very clear: this book will not be filled with man-bashing. In fact, I have to be honest with the ladies… you're not helping the matter. Sometimes, you're even making it worse. Let me explain.

Many of you have lowered your standards when it comes to men. You have settled for far less than God ever intended. This is why some of you woke up one morning, looked at the man in your bed, and thought, *This is who I've linked myself to for the rest of my life? Seriously? What was I thinking?*

Were you thinking that he was all you could expect or deserve in a man?

Another reason many of you aren't helping the 'man problem' is because you've settled for an inferior definition of yourselves. God intends great things for women, but many of you have been listening to the wrong voices. You've been listening to men, other women, culture, and media. The fear of being alone and the voices in your head – born out of past mistakes and choices – have caused you to view yourself as cheap and weak. God says you are none of those things, but you've shut God out.

As a matter of fact, I didn't come up with the name for this book while sitting in the living room with some buddies, watching the game, drinking beer, high-fiving, and laughing at the thought of 'growing a pair'. Instead, I stole it from a group of women at Flatirons Community Church who were brainstorming names for their annual women's retreat. They recognized that something was missing in the lives of women, and they joked about naming the retreat 'Grow A Pair'.

This book uses male examples, but the application taught through these examples applies to both sexes: something is missing in our lives. At Flatirons, we often talk about how, with God in your life and Jesus in your heart, you can become the man or woman you were meant to be. In this book, we are going to go a step deeper. We are going to describe what being a godly man or woman looks like in real life. We are going to give examples of how godly people should act. We are going to reveal how godly people are called to treat themselves and others.

Whether you are a man or a woman, all of the teachings in this book are applicable because they are all based on the presence or absence of 'pairs' in your life. No… we definitely aren't talking about testicles anymore. We are talking about character.

Regardless of the plumbing fixtures God has assigned you, the presence or absence of certain characteristics in your life are issues that we desperately need to address. There are characteristics that, when paired together correctly, will always outweigh and outlast your hormone level, the size of your bank account, or the length of your list of accomplishments, mistakes, and devastations.

Messy stories

Throughout this book, we are going to examine the lives of people found in both the Bible's time and our time.

Some of these people led righteous lives because they relied on the presence of two vital characteristics. Others watched their lives collapse due to the absence of two vital characteristics. We are going to learn from these people and ask ourselves if their particular characteristics play crucial roles in our lives. If the answer is *no*, then we need to find them. We need to reclaim those characteristics. We need to grow a pair.

One of the people we will learn about is Joseph. Joseph's story is in the Bible, and I first learned about him when I was just a kid in Sunday school. He's not the same as the Christmas story guy: Joseph and Mary and baby Jesus and shepherds and little drummer boys and no room in the inn. Instead, the Joseph we are going to talk about lived several hundred years before the whole Bethlehem story took place.

I'll talk about Joseph extensively next chapter, but right now, I want to give you the Sunday school version of his story that I was taught as a kid: Joseph was favored by his father, his brothers were jealous and did some terrible things to him, he went through some hard times, but because he loved God so much, he eventually saved his entire family from starving to death.

Here is the problem with the summarized, Sunday school version of Joseph's story: it has been sanitized. It skips over the messy stuff, and as many of us have experienced, the messy parts of our stories are the most important.

Isn't it true that the most important moments of our lives are not usually the most fun and easy? People's lives don't change when they receive great birthday gifts. People change when they lose something. People change when something or someone is taken from them. Wouldn't you say that the hard, unfair, unclear, and uncertain moments of your life were the moments that most shaped your direction and sense of purpose? Aren't these the moments that keep you up at night? Aren't these the moments that you allow to define your worth?

Life happens during the messy moments, so in the next chapter, we are going to look at the very real and very messy story of a guy named Joseph. Joseph didn't just have a rough day… he had a rough life. He spent the majority of that life wrestling with the voices in his head… trying to determine which ones were worth listening to. The circumstances of his life were lying to Joseph by telling him that he was insignificant and worthless.

Later in this book, we will look at the life of Samson. God gave Samson some powerful attributes and opportunities, but Samson used them in ways that God never intended. We will discover that God might make you strong, but if you don't use that strength in the way he intended, then one day you'll look into your past and see nothing but the strewn bodies of people you've hurt, abused, or left behind.

We will learn about a lesser-known man from the Bible named Boaz. We will learn about a guy named David who was given a chance but blew it. He was given a second chance but blew it again. He was given a third chance but blew it *again*. David repeated this painful process until he died.

Throughout this book, we will study story after story, and we will be able to see ourselves reflected clearly in these stories. Many of us will deeply resonate with them: *That's me. I've done that. I know how that feels. That happened to me. I don't ever want to do that again.*

Many of us will end up asking tough questions: *Where do I go from here? What do I do? Do I have what I need in order to become the man or woman that I was meant to be? If I don't, then what needs to change?*

The answer, of course, is simple: *You need to grow a pair… a pair of characteristics that will allow God to strengthen your life.*

If you've ever had a life-changing, messy moment – whether it occurred last week or fifty years ago – that haunts your thoughts and influences how you treat yourself and those around you… if you can only examine your life through that moment's distorting lens… if you worry that your past is stopping God from using you in the future… then I'll repeat my initial request: *Will you please consider reading the rest of this book?*

Paul

There are two more issues I need to discuss before we can move on and tackle the stories I've just mentioned. First, some of you may be thinking, *I see where you're going with this, Jim… but don't you think this is a little crude? "Grow A Pair"? Really? Isn't that a bit too Jr. High for a 'Christian' book?*

I disagree. More importantly, Paul (one of the most contributive authors of the Bible) would disagree. One time, Paul was listening to some religious people who were teaching that circumcision (ask your mom or doctor) was the only thing that mattered when it came to being a godly man. They were saying that God demanded certain physical attributes before he was willing to use men for his purposes. Paul reacted strongly:

For in Christ Jesus neither circumcision nor uncircumcision has any value. The only thing that counts is faith expressing itself through love. (Galatians 5:6)

Paul was reminding the people that their physical attributes had absolutely nothing to do with being the people

God wanted them to be. Instead, becoming who you were meant to be is based on what you're willing to let God do *through* your life.

The religious people, however, weren't connecting with this concept, so Paul kept ranting:

As for those agitators, I wish they would go the whole way and emasculate themselves! (Galatians 5:12)

Paul pointed at the agitators – those who were claiming physical appearance as a factor in godliness – and said, *You shouldn't stop with circumcision! You should just* (I don't know how else to put this) *go ahead and cut the whole package off!*

Was Paul being crude? Was he being a bit offensive and slightly inappropriate? Absolutely! But he made his point. He did his best to grasp the attention of his listeners and drive home a point that God himself had already made:

The Lord does not look at the things man looks at. Man looks at the outward appearance, but the Lord looks at the heart. (1 Samuel 16:7b)

To be honest, I don't quite care if you find this book's title offensive, immature, or childish because – *TA-DA!* – I got you to pick it up. I'm only trying to drive home the same wisdom Paul offered: your internal attributes are what matter to God, not your external. So… if your internal characteristics truly matter, then do you have the right pairs? If not, do you know how to retrieve them?

Chuck

The second and last issue I need to discuss before moving on is my personal reason for the importance of biblical manhood in my life: my father. This deserves some explanation.

In 2003, when I was still living in Lexington, Kentucky, I picked up my dad (Chuck) from the hospital after he had eye surgery. On the way home, we stopped at a restaurant, and we were engaged in the usual, mundane chitchat: *Did you watch Weather Channel? It's gonna be nice out. What did you order?*

Suddenly, out of the blue, I decided to begin a conversation that my dad and I had never had: *Dad, I don't know anything about your side of the family. I don't know how you grew up. There is a big, blank space in my head when it comes to your life before you met mom.*

Until that day in the restaurant, I had never really thought about my dad's family. Growing up, we only visited my mom's side of the family, and I couldn't have told you all the names of the aunts, uncles, and cousins from my dad's side. I knew almost nothing about my dad's past. He was a pastor, and I didn't even know how he became a Christian.

It took over forty years, but I finally decided to ask my dad to tell his story. For the next couple of hours, my dad relived bits and pieces of his painful history. My jaw was on the table.

Fast-forward seven years. It was 2010, and my parents were in Colorado for my son's wedding. My dad had retired since that night in the restaurant. He and my mom had settled down on the family farm in Indiana, and he did nothing but mow his twenty-five acres of grass and follow the Indianapolis Colts. During their visit, he mentioned that he had been getting really bored. Again, out of the blue, I had an idea.

I told my dad, *Hey, I've got a favor to ask. Remember that night at the restaurant in Lexington? Remember when you told me all those stories from your childhood that I had never heard before?*

He replied, *No?*

I couldn't believe it. *Wait, dad... you don't remember telling me that story about when you were thirteen years old? You said your family couldn't afford a tractor, so you owned two horses and a plow. Remember? You said the horses broke loose in a thunderstorm, and they got tangled up. Grandpa was trying to get them untangled, and he was beating them. Then, he turned to you, started cussing you out, and began beating you instead. You don't remember that?*

Well, I remember the beating, he said. *But I don't remember telling you.*

For the next ten minutes, my dad began telling me every intimate detail of that day in the field. Suddenly, I wasn't sitting next to my dad anymore. I was sitting next to a skinny, shivering thirteen-year-old boy reliving one of the worst moments of his life. Here is my dad's story:

> *I was probably in the seventh grade or somewhere along there. My dad and I were down in the field, and he was beating on the horses. He was trying to get the horses' feet underneath of themselves so they could get out of the ravine. He finally got the horses turned over, and they weren't hurt or anything, but he then turned to me and started beating me with the horse reins... like it was all my fault. All I tried to do was go and help the old guy unhook the horses.*

He gave me a working over down there, and no one ever saw what he did. It's just one of those things that stays with me.

We started up the lane toward the house. When I walked in, I stalked up the stairs – I didn't want to talk to anyone. I stayed up there for several hours until my mom called up for me, "Charles, supper's ready. You'd better come down and eat."

I said to my mother, "I don't care if I never eat another meal in this house."

I immediately thought to myself, "He's gonna come upstairs and kill me this time."

But he never came upstairs. I think he knew he'd gone too far. I think he knew that I would've probably killed him if I could have.

We used to have a family reunion every year. One year, as we were sitting around the table, my brother, Jack – who has never been known for his finesse – said, "Oh... I remember when dad gave you a workin' over," and all of the conversation in the room stopped. Everyone knew I had had troubles adjusting to my family ever since that day in the field.

After Jack said that, it all came back to me with the storm, my father beating me with the reins, and everything. I looked at Jack, and I said, "That night, if I could've gotten a gun... you would have been without a father." I wouldn't have been without a father because I had already denounced him as my father at that point.

Those things still come back to you.

In fact, I remember always feeling that my ministry as a pastor was handicapped because I would tell others that they had to forgive their enemies, and yet, I could never forgive my dad.

During my dad's visit to Colorado in 2010, I asked if he would let me capture some of his story. In the end, he agreed. I flew to Indiana, and a crew from Flatirons filmed my dad as he told his story. We used the footage to compliment the *Grow A Pair* teachings at Flatirons, and the section above is the written adaptation of that footage. [2]

Initially, my dad was confused by the favor: *Why would I ever want to write that story down? Why would I ever want to keep that particular story?*

I told him what was on my heart. *Why? Because it's your story, and I never want to lose it. It's a story of redemption… it's a 'Flatirons story'. It's a story about how God can take someone – regardless of their pain and their past – and he can use them to do great things, just like God has used you to do great things.*

Then, he said it…

He said, *I've never done anything great with my life… the only good thing to come out of my life is you and your sister.*

I couldn't believe what I was hearing. I told him, *Dad, the only reason I'm a good pastor is because you were a good pastor!*

He replied, *I wasn't a good pastor… I was a hypocrite. I*

told people to forgive those who had hurt them, but I have never been able to forgive my father for what he did to my family and me.

Then, it clicked. I realized that my 77-year-old dad was still wrestling with and being defined by something that happened more than sixty years ago. He was having trouble seeing that his past *is* what made him a great pastor. Because of his story, he was able to look out at people and say, *Me too…*

In the next chapter, we will look more at the messy story of a guy named Joseph. We will also look more at the messy story of a guy named Chuck – a guy who I just call 'Dad' – because you've only seen the tip of the iceberg.

Throughout the rest of this book, we are going to look at the stories of men who never quit trying. Sometimes, they did well. Other times, they screwed up. But… they never quit trying. My hope is that you will see your story reflected somewhere in this book. My hope is that, as you read, you will be able to say, *Me too…*

1. For a whole book about the differences between men and women discussed in the Bible, check out our sermon series book entitled *PB&J: Key Ingredients for a Better Marriage*.

2. The videos of my dad are available for viewing under the "Resources: Listen/Watch Messages" tab at www.flatironschurch.com. Watch Week One of *Grow A Pair* (September 11-12, 2010).

01. Grow A Pair... Of What?
General Discussion Questions

Core:

1. What were your initial thoughts when you first read this book's title?

2. Can you remember a specific situation in which you've heard someone use the term 'grow a pair'?

3. Are there any particular characteristics in others that you find admirable? What are they?

4. What do you remember the most from your childhood about your father?

5. Do you think the definition of manhood has changed over the last few generations?

6. Do you think most peoples' perceptions of Jesus could be described as 'manly'? Why or why not?

7. Do you agree that most churches today offer an unspoken message that men must surrender their manhood, spine, and personality in order to become a follower of Jesus?

8. In what ways do men use church and the Bible to bully and intimidate others?

9. How would you describe the type of man that God desires a woman to seek?

10. Why do you think some women settle for men who don't live up to God's standards for manhood?

11. What are some of today's cultural misconceptions about men and women?

12. Read Genesis 50:20. Do you *really* believe God can accomplish good things through bad circumstances? If so, how have you witnessed this in your own life?

13. Read Galatians 5:6 and 5:12. Are you offended by Paul's language in these verses?

14. In reference to Galatians 5:6 and 5:12, have you ever had 'agitators' in your life? What did they try to force you to do? What did they try to force you *not* to do?

15. Read 1 Samuel 16:7. What do you think God looks for in women and men? What do you think most men look for in a woman and vice versa?

16. What did you think of Chuck's story about his abusive father? Did it remind you of a story of your own? Do you know someone who is plagued and defined by his or her past? Are *you* tormented and defined by your past?

Challenge:

1. Meditate on Genesis 50:20, and try to see where God may have used your past struggles and mistakes to accomplish something good.

2. Take an honest, personal inventory, and determine the character traits you possess that you think God can use for his purposes. Determine the character traits you possess that you think God wants you to change.

01. Grow A Pair... Of What?
Discussion Questions for Women

Core:

1. How has the idea of the 'sameness' of men and women affected the way women view themselves? How has this concept affected the way men view women? In general, how has this concept affected relationships between men and women?

2. Do you believe that men in our culture are functioning in ways that God never intended? If so, has this made women function in ways that God never intended?

3. What are some of the standards our culture uses to assess women?

4. In Genesis 50:20, Joseph reflects on the terrible things done to him throughout his life, and he discusses how God has used those things for good. Do you have a story about God taking tragedy and pain in your life and using it for good?

5. Do women have more of a tendency than men to develop an attitude of victimization? If so, how can a relationship with God change that?

6. Read Galatians 5:6. What's the meaning in this verse for women? How would you translate this verse to speak specifically to women?

7. What are some specific stories you've heard from women that have helped you formulate your concept of womanhood? Have you heard any stories that have skewed your understanding of what it means to 'be a woman'?

8. How would you describe the type of man that God desires a woman to seek?

9. Why do you think some women settle for men who don't live up to God's standards for manhood?

10. If you could give one piece of advice to a young woman in your life (daughter, niece, granddaughter, friend, etc.) about what it means to 'be a woman', what would you say?

Challenge:

1. Make a date to sit down and talk with a woman you value. Share stories of events in your lives that have shaped you as women.

2. Take some time to write down the areas in your life where your self-image may not match up with God's image of you. Ask God to allow you to see his vision of you.

02.
Joseph and Chuck... Identity and Integrity

By
Jim Burgen

02.
Joseph and Chuck... Identity and Integrity

Some of us are listening to the wrong voices. Even though God is the only person who has the ability to define our worth and value, we choose to ignore him and opt for the pervasive voices of our culture. God says:

The Lord does not look at the things man looks at. Man looks at the outward appearance, but the Lord looks at the heart. (1 Samuel 16:7b)

For some destructive reason, we continue to listen to the voices of the world. Culture tries to convince us that our external attributes give us our worth and value – our jobs, our incomes, our cars, our physical appearances, and our past mistakes – but God says that he doesn't care about any of those things. God cares about our hearts. God cares about our character.

Oftentimes, the types of characteristics that God desires exist in pairs. To understand our first pair of crucial, godly characteristics, we are going to examine the lives of the two men I briefly mentioned in the last chapter: Joseph and my dad, Chuck. I want to look at these two stories simultaneously because they have many parallels. They are both messy and frustrating stories, but they are also hopeful stories of God's redemption.

Joseph – A man without a home

The story of Joseph is one of those stories that I've never quite understood. Don't get me wrong. I've heard it thousands of times since Sunday school, and I can recite the entire story from front to back, but at the same time, I've never understood the story. Here's what I mean: if I were in Joseph's shoes, I would not have been able to reach the profound levels of wisdom and forgiveness that he displayed. He was a much better man than I will ever be.

Last chapter, I gave you the Sunday school version of Joseph's story. Now, let's hear the messy version. [1] Joseph was a seventeen-year-old boy who lived during the Bible's times. Joseph's family was huge. His dad was on his third marriage, so Joseph had eleven half-brothers from three different moms. This family was what we, in the 21st century, like to call a 'blended family'.

Joseph's dad favored Joseph. Not only did he favor Joseph, but he also made his favoritism incredibly apparent to the rest of the family. He would come home and gaze at his twelve sons, but give gifts only to Joseph. I'm sure this treatment is great… if you're the favorite. If you are one of the remaining family members… I'll bet it sucks.

This treatment began going to Joseph's head. Sometimes, he mouthed off. Sometimes, his actions were arrogant and self-involved. He wasn't too humble, but he was mostly just acting like a teenage boy. Who knows? Maybe he had recently received his camel-driving license, and all of the cruises through town had made him cocky? I'm not sure if that's historically accurate, but anyway…

One morning at breakfast, Joseph felt especially sure of himself, and he decided to share a dream with his family that he probably should have kept to himself: *Hey guys, put down your forks! Everybody listen! You've got to hear this! Last night, I had a dream. In it, God told me that I'm going to be famous! Like a superstar! And there's more... he said that all of you guys are going to bow down to the ground before me! Isn't that awesome! Could you pass the potatoes, please?*

Joseph felt good. Life was great. Everything was smooth sailing. Joseph had big plans for his life. More importantly, *God* had big plans for Joseph's life.

Remember that... because Joseph had no idea what was coming next.

The dream didn't go over well with Joseph's brothers. They had had enough. After breakfast, the brothers held a secret meeting in the backyard, and they decided to finally take care of their pesky brother. A few days later, when dad was out of town, Joseph's brothers called him out to a field. *Hey, why don't you come with us, little dreamer boy?*

They proceeded to beat Joseph within an inch of his life. After the beating, they threw him down a well in order to keep Joseph contained while they figured out a plan to cover up his murder. While Joseph was in the well, one of the brothers developed a bright idea: *Let's not murder him... let's make some money off of him!*

They sold Joseph into slavery, took his coat (a precious gift from his father), smeared it with goat's blood, took it home to their father, and told their dad that a bear killed Joseph. I'll bet, at Joseph's funeral, the brothers stole away hidden high-fives and muffled laughter. This family was what we, in the 21st century, like to call a 'dysfunctional blended family'.

What must Joseph be thinking *now*? Just days ago, he was on top of the world. Life looked like a piece of cake. He was convinced that God had a plan of fame and power for his life. Now, he has been nearly murdered by his brothers and sold into slavery.

Where is God in all of this?

Chuck – A man without a home

> *I started going to church when I was in high school. At first, I went to a Baptist church because one of my best friends, Dave Smith, went there. My dad was a friend with Dave's family, and Dave and I became real good friends. In fact, we were like brothers… we really loved one another.*
>
> *Then, Dave went off to Korea and got killed…*
>
> *On one particular day – a Friday it was – I had made arrangements to go on a date with a girl. I was double dating with a buddy, and the girl was going to bring a friend and everything, so I was real excited about that. I told my dad that we needed to get home because I had a date, but Friday was always a payday for my dad, and he always had to go to this bar. I was waiting in the car for him, but he stayed and he stayed and he stayed…*
>
> *Finally, I went in and said, "Dad, we really got to get going."*
>
> *Well, he was really angry that I'd pushed him that way. So… I'm driving a little fast to get home*

because I was late, and he said, "You'd better slow this #$! thing down or we're going to get a ticket!"*

I said, "If I get a ticket, I'll pay for it." I was so mad at him.

So... he started telling me how worthless I was and how I didn't appreciate anything. We were driving along this road, and out of the blue, he said to me, "I hope you go to Korea and get your #$! head blown off."*

I just said, "Well, you know, if I do... then I won't have to be around people like you."

That really set him off. I was behind the wheel, but he grabbed for me, ripped my shirt off, and tore me across the chest. He started hitting on me and everything, and I knew I had to get away from him. I got off to the shoulder of the road, jumped out, and ran away from him.

I later found out that he had gone and gotten a gun, and he went out hunting for me...

I don't know what I did right after that. There's a big blank space about where I stayed and everything. But I never went home again... [2]

Joseph – A man at the end of his rope

Joseph was put on a wagon and hauled off to Egypt. In Egypt, a rich guy named Potiphar purchased Joseph to be his servant – a personal butler. Potiphar was a man of power because he worked for Pharaoh, the king. Joseph worked really hard; so hard that he gradually rose his way through the slave ranks to become in charge of Potiphar's money and investments. Joseph lived and worked in Potiphar's home and became very close with the family. However, Joseph's position at the home created a problem. Potiphar's wife decided she wanted to cheat on her husband with Joseph. Joseph continually refused her advances, but she wouldn't quit:

(6) Now Joseph was well-built and handsome, (7) and after a while his master's wife took notice of Joseph and said, "Come to bed with me!"
(8) But he refused. "With me in charge," he told her, "my master does not concern himself with anything in the house; everything he owns he has entrusted to my care. (9) No one is greater in this house than I am. My master has withheld nothing from me except you, because you are his wife. How then could I do such a wicked thing and sin against God?" (10) And though she spoke to Joseph day after day, he refused to go to bed with her or even be with her. (Genesis 39:6b-10)

Joseph told Potiphar's wife that he would not sin against God, which reveals that Joseph was still holding out hope in God's promise for a future. But... even though Joseph fought off her advances, his bright future refused to show itself. Potiphar's wife became angry with Joseph for his constant denials, so she falsely accused him of rape, and Joseph was sent to prison for a crime he did not commit.

In prison, Joseph shared a jail block with two guys who used to work for Pharaoh. The two guys began having some really strange dreams, so they asked Joseph what they meant because God had given Joseph the ability to interpret dreams.

Joseph looked at the first guy and said, *Hmmm, that's rough. Sorry, that's a bad dream. It means you're going to die.*

Then, Joseph looked at the second guy and said, *Okay! Your dream is better! You are going to get out of prison, get your job back, and stand in front of the king! Hey, by the way, when you stand in front of Pharaoh, will you please remember me? Will you put in a good word for me? I'm not supposed to be here. I was wrongly accused. Please, remember me. Please, help me out. Do you promise?*

The guy said thanks, promised to help Joseph, was released from prison, and immediately forgot about him.

Once again, what must Joseph be thinking *now*? He has lost his family, his job, his reputation, and his freedom. He has been accused of crimes he never committed. He is alone in a strange place.

Where is God in all of this?

Chuck – A man at the end of his rope

> *Within days, I was on a bus going to Fort Riley, Kansas to take my basic training. The Army kind of became my home for a while. It was during the time I was in Korea that I decided I wanted to become a minister. The two years went by quite fast, and I could see God's hand so many times.*
>
> *On Christmas Eve, I was on a ship going over to Korea from Fort Lewis, Washington. I don't know if the ship broke down or what, but they turned off the motors, and we were out there alone in the middle of the ocean.*

I went up on the deck, and I was kind of depressed because I was without family. Here it was, Christmas Eve, and I was going to Korea – I didn't know what was going to happen there.

So... I went up on the deck of this troop ship on Christmas Eve, and it was just as black as it could be out there. I even thought about jumping over because I was so depressed. But I was leaning over the deck, and I saw the stars and everything... and it was just like you could reach out – it was one of those magic moments for me – it was just like you could reach out and touch God... it was like God spoke to me and said, "Chuck, it's going to be okay... it's going to be okay."

And I felt a peace that came. And I knew it was going to be okay...

Joseph – A man saved by grace

Joseph sat in prison for thirteen years. Not thirteen weeks... not thirteen months... but thirteen years. Eventually, Pharaoh had a dream that no one could decipher, and Joseph's former cellmate finally remembered him. He told Pharaoh about Joseph, and Joseph was called before the king. Joseph immediately explained Pharaoh's dream: *Pharaoh, your dream means that your land is going to have seven more years of great crop. But after those seven years, you are going to have another seven years of great famine and drought. Here's what I would do... I'd store up the next seven years' worth of food so that, when the famine finally strikes, people will come to you to buy food. You'll get rich.*

Pharaoh loved the idea and ended up putting Joseph in command of the entire operation. He freed Joseph from prison, put him in charge of the country's food and money, gave him a mansion, gave him a wife, and made him rich. At thirty years old, Joseph's life was starting to look up.

Needless to say, Joseph's interpretation of Pharaoh's dream came true. Under Joseph's leadership, the Egyptians built bigger barns to store extra crops. Then, after seven years of perfect weather, the rains ceased, the sun continued to beat down, and the land died. People from all over this part of the world hopped in their wagons and rode toward Egypt. When they reached Egypt, they entered a palace, bowed down before Joseph's throne, and begged to buy food from the nation's massive supply.

A few years into the devastating famine, guess who showed up to bow down before Joseph and beg for food? His brothers.

The brothers didn't even recognize Joseph. In fact, seeing Joseph was the furthest thought from their minds. Twenty-five years ago, they sold their brother into slavery, and slaves rarely lived for long. If they ever took the time to think about Joseph, they probably thought about how he was dead. So the brothers didn't recognize Joseph… but you'd better believe that Joseph recognized them.

What must Joseph be thinking *now*? I know what would be going through my head: *I remember you… as a matter of fact, the last time I saw you guys, you were punching my lights out. Then, you sold me into slavery like a dog you didn't want anymore. In a single day, I lost my parents, my brothers, my home, and my freedom. You took everything from me. And by the way, it was no accident. You did this on purpose! Because of what you did to me, I've been a slave, I've been wrongly accused of rape, and I've* *spent thirteen years in prison. And now... when things are finally looking good... you guys show up and expect me to help you? Listen closely because I've been rehearsing this speech for years: #*$! YOU! What goes around comes around! Look who's bowing down to Joseph! Look who's the man!*

That's what I would have said to those murderous, betraying brothers, but thankfully, Joseph was a better man than I'll ever be. He didn't immediately explode in fury at his brothers. He didn't use his power to enact revenge. He didn't act on any of those violent impulses, but that doesn't mean he wasn't tempted. In fact, the more I read this story, the more I realize how emotionally and internally mixed up Joseph was when he saw his brothers. Three different times during the encounter, Joseph had to run out of the room crying, and I'll bet it wasn't because he was overwhelmed with joy. No... he was an emotional wreck because he had a tug-of-war going on inside his heart. *Do I forgive them... or do I pay them back?*

Joseph wrestled with this concept for a long time, but finally, he kicked everyone out of the room except for his brothers. He looked into their faces and said, *It's me. It's Joseph... the brother you betrayed.*

You have to think that this was an '*Oh Crap!*' moment for the brothers. First of all, you cannot simply forget about selling your own brother into slavery. These brothers remembered what they had done. Second, the brothers knew exactly what they deserved, and third, the brothers knew how they would've reacted in Joseph's position. They believed their pathetic lives were over.

But Joseph didn't end his brothers' lives. Somehow, Joseph sensed the hugeness of that moment. He contemplated the strange irony of his brothers now begging for his help, and Joseph realized that something special was happening in his life – something bigger than betrayal, and something greater than revenge. In the end, Joseph not only forgave his brothers, but he also fed them. Listen to Joseph's words:

> **(19) But Joseph said to them, "Don't be afraid. Am I in the place of God? (20) You intended to harm me, but God intended it for good to accomplish what is now being done, the saving of many lives. (21) So then, don't be afraid. I will provide for you and your children." And he reassured them and spoke kindly to them. (Genesis 50:19-21)**

Now, I'll be honest… the first thousand times I read this story, I thought, *Bad idea, Joseph. You're letting them off way too easy. At least, punch them! Anything!*

But the more I come to understand this story, the more I love Joseph for what he *didn't* say. He didn't say, *Oh, it's okay. Let's just forget about the whole thing.* Instead, Joseph called out the situation for what it was. Joseph reminded his brothers that they intended harm, they wronged him, and they intentionally discarded him. He was honest about his story: *Listen… you guys got together, formed a plan, took notes, threw me into a well, and sold me into slavery… on purpose! But God* (those words change everything) *intended to take your horrible actions and use them to accomplish something wonderful. Your actions were still horrible, and what you did to me will never be okay. But God is not going to waste those actions. Instead, he's going to use them. You don't need to be afraid of me because I'm not going to take revenge on you… that's God's job. I'll give you what you need rather than what you deserve.*

Do you know what I call Joseph's reaction? I call it *unfair*! We learn the terms 'fair' and 'unfair' at a very early age. When he got two cookies, but you only got one… that was *unfair*! When you ran the race, but she got the medal… that was *unfair*! We love 'fairness' when we are on the right side of the deal. When we are being rewarded or enjoying satisfaction, then we love 'fairness', but when we are on the *wrong* side, 'fairness' is the last thing we want because we don't want what we genuinely deserve.

The biblical term for this type of unfairness is 'grace'. There are two different types of grace. The first is the type of grace that forgives someone despite the fact that they deserve to be punished. This is the type of grace that everyone wants to receive from God. *Please God, don't give me what I deserve. Please, be unfair.*

The other type of grace looks like this: *'Grace' is the strength that God promises to give us in order to do something we could never do on our own.* I'm talking about the kind of strength that can only be explained by God. Some of us (like Joseph) have lived through situations so impossibly difficult that the only explanation for why we are still living and surviving is because God gave us the *grace* (strength) to survive.

This is the amazing type of grace that God gave Joseph, and this is the amazing type of grace that God offers to all of his people. This is the type of grace that makes it possible to survive the train wrecks of our lives.

Identity and integrity

Over the years, the story of Joseph has gradually revealed a truth to me. The truth doesn't have to do with Joseph. Instead, the truth has to do with something Jesus said a long time ago. One time, Jesus said, *If someone strikes you on the cheek, then don't strike them back, but offer your other cheek as well.*[3] I used to wish he hadn't said that. I hated that teaching… but only because I didn't fully understand what Jesus meant.

First, let me explain what Jesus *wasn't* saying. He wasn't saying, *If you love me, then let people slap you around. If you want to be a good little Christian, then be a doormat. Let people take advantage of you. Don't protect yourself. It doesn't matter if you get slapped in the face – I don't care.*

That is *not* what Jesus was saying.

Jesus was saying something different. He was saying, *When you get slapped or punched in the face… physically, emotionally, relationally… when someone intentionally hurts you, insults you, degrades you, embarrasses you, molests you, rapes you, devastates your life… you need to be the person who says, "Enough! This has to stop somewhere, and it stops with me. This has been going on for generations in my family, but not anymore. I am ending the generational trend of cheek-slapping, eye-gouging, teeth-knocking, wife-beating, child-abusing, heart-crushing, life-ruining violence."*

In other words, your dad might have been abusive because *his* dad was abusive, but you could be the one to stop the trend. Your dad might have been a terrible father, *but you are not your dad*. Your mom might have been a terrible mother, *but you are not your mom*.

With God's strength, you don't have to continue your family's destructive traditions.

Most of us don't realize the destruction in our lives until we pause to glance in the rearview mirror. Only when we pause to look back do we see all of the effort that we poured into paying people back and punishing our enemies. Only then do we see all of the mistakes we made during faulty attempts to heal our own wounds. Only then do we realize that we were merely getting stoned or drunk to try to pretend our problems didn't matter. Only then do we realize that our attempts to heal our wounds did nothing but dominate and define our lives. These attempts only ripped us off and ruined other people's lives.

There's a certain irony that comes with this honest reflection because, even after the ability to look back and identify the mistakes in your life, you are still left with the same question: *What do I do with what happened to me? I can't change it, undo it, or deny it, so what do I do now?*

The answer is, *You need to grow a pair.*

This does *not* mean that you need to 'man up', 'toughen up', 'suck it up', or 'get over' the damage you've been dealt. God will never say that to you, and you will never hear that ideology preached in this book. When I say, *You need to grow a pair*, I mean that you need to find and reconnect with a pair of characteristics that will aid in changing your life. There are many pairs of characteristics that are vital, but the characteristics that are most strongly portrayed in this chapter's stories are *identity* and *integrity*.

Let me explain these terms. *Identity* means you have to find a higher, better, purer source – one that isn't based on the ever-changing circumstances of your life – to be a voice that reminds you of who you are and what you're worth. Once you've come to believe in that voice, then you must choose to live a life that is consistent with that voice's definition of your worth and value; this is called *integrity*: living a life that is consistent with your identity.

The word 'integrity' means, "one; linked together; or, inseparable." In other words, you can only be one person: *If I think I am like that, then naturally, I will act like that.* When we find our identities in the wrong places, we begin to live with a skewed sense of integrity. If someone in your life says you're stupid, you're worthless, and you don't matter… and if you begin to *believe* those things… then that's your identity. Next, you will start to live a life that is consistent with that identity. You will live a life of stupidity, worthlessness, and uselessness.

Identity and *integrity*. How does this pair of characteristics factor into your life?

I truly believe that I'm a worthless, stupid failure… so that's exactly how I choose to live. Why not fail again? I'm a failure. Why not get high or drunk again? I'm a drunk. Why not walk out on my family? I'm a quitter.

If enough people treat you like a punching bag… if enough people treat you like a whore… if enough people call you certain names; names like *loser*, *wimp*, *queer*, *faggot*… then eventually, you begin to believe them, right?

Some of us have been listening to the wrong voices, and (worst of all) we have chosen to see ourselves in light of those voices' descriptions. We treat ourselves poorly, and we allow others to treat us poorly.

If I stopped this chapter right here, then this would be the most depressing book ever written. But there *must* be a better way. Surely, we aren't doomed to be defined by the circumstances of our pasts. Surely, we aren't condemned to live our lives based on those circumstances.

There *is* a better way! There is a better, higher, purer voice, and that is the voice of God. God says, *I'm the one who gets to tell you who you are. I'm the one who gets to tell you what you're worth. I want you to live a better life that is based on my definition. Regardless of what anyone has ever said to you or done to you, this is who you are:*

You are my child, and I am your father. [4]

You are forgiven from every sin and mistake you've ever made because of my son, Jesus. [5]

You are free from all condemnation. [6]

You are a new creation… the old 'you' is gone. [7]

I don't hate you. I love you. [8]

You aren't a victim of this corrupt world. Instead, you are part of a higher, divine world. [9]

That is the voice of God. That is who you are meant to be. The only reason this definition of your life sounds impossible is because you've been listening to the wrong voices for far too long. God says that if you will only turn your ear toward him, then you'll hear the truth. Jesus says if you will hold onto that truth and live by its wisdom, then you will be set free. Free from the lies you've been buying into for years. Free to become the man or woman you were meant to be. Free to be the person God says you are.

Don't you want to be free?

Chuck – A man saved by grace

I've read other writers who have taught this same message of truth and love, and I've thought to myself, *That's great for most people, but I know myself too well. I know who I am and what I've done. I want to be that man, but I can't… I still feel guilty… I still feel condemned. Logically, it doesn't make sense that God loves me and forgives me.*

I know that feeling. I know that this doesn't make any logical sense, but most of the time, God and logic don't always go together. A lot of times, God is very illogical.

For example, if you want to talk logic, then my dad ought to be an alcoholic like his dad. Instead, my dad never drank a drop while I was growing up. My dad ought to be an abusive husband and father like his dad. Instead, my dad never laid a finger on any of us in anger. My dad ought to be an angry, bitter man. Would you blame him? Instead, my dad is responsible for teaching thousands of people about Jesus. He allowed countless numbers of people to sleep on our couch or spare bed when they were in trouble. He's responsible for getting me to stand on a stage week after week and talk about how God loves us.

This doesn't make sense. My dad's behavior is illogical. But… that doesn't matter because, at some point, my dad stopped listening to his earthly father – who was lying – and started listening to his heavenly Father. At some point, my dad chose to find his identity in God and live that new life with integrity.

I don't know if my dad has totally forgiven his own father for the horrible things he was made to suffer… all I know is that my dad is *not* who my grandpa tried to tell him he was:

> *When I look over my life, I didn't know there was another way to live until I met a minister who took me under his wing. He showed me what kindness was. He gave me a vision and he gave me hope. There have been a lot of people who have helped me along the way, and God is good - you know the old saying: "Life is hard, but God is good."*

One of my favorite sayings used to be John 3:16, but you have to go on and include verses seventeen and eighteen because God didn't come to punish us or judge us. He came to give us life everlasting.

In God, I found a father I never had or never knew. He's a good father, and I love him. He's blessed me in so many ways.

* * * * * *

My dad's story and Joseph's story are the same, and many of us can see our stories reflected in theirs. Joseph was treated like garbage, but God believed he was better than that. Joseph had a horrible life; who would have blamed him for seeking a little comfort from Potiphar's wife? But Joseph's response was, *How could I sin against God like that? Even if people treat me like a slave, I'm not. I belong to God.*

If Joseph allowed his circumstances to dictate his identity, then logically, he should have paid his brothers back for everything they had done to him. However, if he acted logically, he only would have proved that his brothers still had power over his life. He only would have proved that his brothers continued to determine his worth and value. Instead, Joseph chose to listen to a different voice.

Can you? Can you listen to a different voice?

Someday, you might be able to forgive some of the damaging people in your past, but I promise that you'll never be able to fully move on until you begin to see yourself in the identity that God declares.

God wants to change your identity. He wants you to say, *I am God's son and he is my father. I am forgiven for every sin and mistake I've ever made because of Jesus. I am free from all condemnation. I am not who I used to be. I am a new creation. God loves me. God promises that I don't have to be a victim of this corrupt world. Instead, I get to be a part of a higher, divine world. I am free.*

I'm not saying you totally believe that yet. But… if you *did*… would it make a difference in your life?

Don't you want to be free?

1. Joseph's entire story can be found in Genesis 37-50.

2. Once again, the videos of my dad's story can be found under the "Resources: Listen/Watch Messages" tab at www.flatironschurch.com. Watch Week Two of *Grow A Pair* (September 18-19, 2010).

3. Matthew 5:39; Luke 6:29.

4. 1 John 3:1-2.

5. Ephesians 1:4-8.

6. Romans 8:1-2.

7. 2 Corinthians 5:17.

8. John 3:16.

9. 2 Peter 1:4.

02. Joseph and Chuck... Identity and Integrity
General Discussion Questions

Core:

1. What does God look for in a man? What does culture typically look for in a man? How do the two differ?

2. Which aspect of Joseph's life do you identify with the most?

3. Did you respond to Joseph's story of identity, integrity, grace, and forgiveness with, *I'm definitely not there yet*? If so, what steps might you begin taking in order to reach that place?

4. What are you not ready to let go of just yet?

5. With whom do you resonate the most: Joseph, the innocent man who had been taken advantage of, or Joseph's brothers, the men who had used their power to take advantage of others?

6. What do you find most amazing about Joseph's story?

7. What do you find most amazing about Chuck's story?

8. What do you find most amazing about your own story?

9. Have the characteristics of 'identity' and 'integrity' played a crucial role in your life? If so, how? If not, why?

10. Over the course of your life, have you ever allowed the wrong voices to define you?

11. Over the course of your life, have you ever started acting on behalf of the wrong identity?

12. Have you ever witnessed God's amazing grace in your life? If so, what did his grace look like?

Challenge:

- Read Genesis 37-50. As you track through Joseph's story, pause to write down moments in your own life that have similarities to Joseph's.

02. Joseph and Chuck... Identity and Integrity Discussion Questions for Women

Core:

1. Are you missing any characteristics in the individual roles you play (wife, mother, daughter, sister, friend, etc.)?

2. What does it look like to 'be a woman' in the world today? What are the standards we use to measure success?

3. Read 1 Samuel 16:7. What are the standards God uses to measure success? Are those standards the same for both men and women?

4. After reading the story of Joseph, what is the first word that comes to your mind when trying to describe his life?

5. Read Genesis 50:20. Did God cause the pain and agony that Joseph endured throughout his life? What did Joseph mean when he said, *You intended to harm me, but God intended it for good to accomplish what is now being done, the saving of many lives*?

6. Have you survived a painful experience that continues to define your life? Have you ever witnessed God take a horrible experience and use it in a positive way?

7. Review the following verses: 1 John 3:1-2; Ephesians 1:6-8; Romans 8:1; 2 Corinthians 5:17; John 3:16; 2 Peter 1:4. In our culture, is the search for identity different for women than it is for men? In God's words, how are men and women's identities similar or different?

8. Is it harder to believe in God's version of identity than the versions projected by your mother, father, husband, boyfriend, etc? Do you trust what God says to be true?

9. If you trusted God's version of your identity and lived that definition with integrity, how would your life change?

Challenge:

- Make a list of the people, circumstances, mistakes, etc. that have spoken into your life and defined your identity. Do any of these things contradict God's offered identity? If so, which ones? Rewrite the list so that it reflects the identity God offers. Ask God to help you see yourself through his eyes.

03.
Samson and Vinnie... Strength and Wisdom

By
Scott Nickell

03.
Samson and Vinnie... Strength and Wisdom

When I was a kid, I was obsessed with the sport of boxing. My dad would buy me old videos of fights from Muhammad Ali, Joe Frazier, and George Foreman. I had a bunch of these famous fights memorized, round for round; fights like *Thrilla in Manila* and *Rumble in the Jungle*. During the Mike Tyson years, boxing became even more exciting, but after Tyson went off the deep end, the sport gradually lost its popular hold in both the nation and also my own life.

In the last decade, a new sport has taken its place and replaced that lost sense of excitement: MMA (mixed martial arts). One of the most prestigious MMA training facilities, Grudge Training Center, is located in Denver, so there are a lot of fighters who spend time in Colorado. A friend of mine, Vinnie Lopez, is a professional MMA fighter who trains at Grudge and also attends Flatirons. Before working on *Grow A Pair*, I had the opportunity to spend a day training and working out with Vinnie. His daily routine is incredibly disciplined, arduous, and exhausting, but those same qualities have played a crucial role in Vinnie's life. Those qualities have helped him become a better father and a better man of God.

Vinnie's story, in part, has inspired the content of this chapter's discussion. He's a great example of a true Christian man – a man who understands he doesn't have to surrender his strength and manhood at the door of the church. A man who understands that, when combining strength and wisdom, you can make manhood and a relationship with God coexist. In fact, God desires this coexistence of strength and wisdom.

Another inspiration for this discussion on strength and wisdom comes from the many Flatirons men's retreats that I've had the chance to attend. At these retreats, 400 men descend on Crooked Creek Ranch near Winter Park, Colorado and have an absolute blast. Here's what you'll see at a typical Flatirons men's retreat (I won't describe *everything* you might see… that could be incriminating): you'll see men fly fishing, hiking, playing basketball, smoking cigars, mountain biking, lifting weights, playing poker, playing dodgeball, or jumping from a thirty-foot platform into a freezing cold lake. But here's the cool thing: you will *also* see these same men singing worship songs loudly to their creator, God. You will see these same men studying scripture, praying, having tough and honest conversations with one another about their struggles, and making renewed commitments to their wives, kids, jobs, and schools. In other words, you will see a bunch of *real* men in action.

Both Vinnie and the men on those retreats have found a way to make their manhood and their relationships with God live in harmony. This is primarily due to the balance of certain attributes and characteristics in their lives. These pairs of qualities make a genuine relationship with God possible. Once again, in order to illustrate this point, we're going to examine the lives of two men: Samson from the Bible and Vinnie from Denver.

Samson – Strength without wisdom

If you grew up in church, then you probably heard the story of Samson every other weekend in Sunday school. The repetition of this story is not without reason. Sunday school teachers learn very quickly that, if you want to engage the minds of young boys, then you need to keep telling stories about people like Samson. Samson's story is an exciting, action-packed tale. However, like the story of Joseph, the Sunday school version of Samson's life is G-rated and sanitized. At Flatirons, we don't sanitize, so if you have any preconceived notions about the story of Samson… throw them away.

Samson's story is found in the Book of Judges, and it's a tale that needs some quick historical background.[1] Samson was an Israelite (one of God's chosen people), and the Israelites had a bad habit: they would walk after God, obey his commands, and believe in his promises, but then, they would eventually grow overconfident, turn their backs on God, and begin worshipping false gods. They continually repeated this cycle between belief and disbelief, and during Samson's time (around 1,000 BC), the Israelites had found themselves in a terrible place. They were occupied by a people group known as the Philistines. The Philistines were ruthless warriors; not only did they love to fight, but they were very, *very* good at it. So… during their time of oppression, the Israelites continued their historically proven cycle of belief, and began begging God for help.

I can't judge the Israelites because I have a very similar pattern in my own life, and maybe you can identify. I have a tendency to follow my own plan despite knowing what is best. Then, when I start to suffer the natural consequences of those actions, I run to God and beg for his help. But… here is something amazing about the nature of God: even though his people repeatedly betray him, God stands right next to them when they cry for help. This quality of God has repeatedly revealed itself in my life, and the Israelites were no different.

So… upon hearing the cries of the Israelites, God raised up a new leader to deliver them from their oppressors: Samson. Samson was a unique person from the very moment he was conceived. First, his mother had been completely unable to have a baby until she miraculously gave birth to Samson. Second, God commanded that Samson be a Nazirite from birth to death.

The word 'nazirite' means, "dedicated or consecrated; set apart for a specific purpose." Sometimes, the Hebrew people would take a 'nazirite vow' for a temporary period of time – sometimes weeks, sometimes months, and sometimes years. The nazirite vow had three main components: (1) you vowed not to drink alcohol, (2) you vowed not to cut your hair, and (3) you vowed not to come near anything dead. The nazirite vow was supposed to be a metaphor or a demonstration of an individual's commitment to God above everything else in the world.

Samson's nazirite vow was unique for a couple of reasons. First, he was set apart from birth to be a Nazirite, so he didn't choose the vow for himself. Second, Samson was commanded to remain a Nazirite for his entire life rather than temporarily. Because of the uniqueness of his nazirite vow, people viewed Samson as an especially devout, committed, disciplined, pious, and self-controlled Hebrew. However, as we've been learning throughout this book, we tend to judge people based on their outward appearances, but God is perceptive enough to understand our true hearts.

Let's walk through Samson's story because we're about to see that his heart needed some serious work.

(1) Samson went down to Timnah and saw there a

young Philistine woman. (2) When he returned, he said to his father and mother, "I have seen a Philistine woman in Timnah; now get her for me as my wife." (Judges 14:1-2)

We immediately see a massive red flag in terms of Samson's character. He entered an area occupied by Philistines and found a woman that he wanted to take as his wife. Despite the fact that the Philistines worshipped another God and were oppressing Samson's people, Samson wanted to take a Philistine wife. In Samson, we immediately see a disregard for God and God's people.

His father and mother replied, "Isn't there an acceptable woman among your relatives or among all our people? Must you go to the uncircumcised Philistines to get a wife?"
But Samson said to his father, "Get her for me. She's the right one for me." (Judges 14:3)

Samson's parents pushed back. Sure… they asked if Samson had considered any of his own relatives, but maybe they were originally from Kentucky (I can make that joke… I spent a lot of my life in Kentucky). The point is that his parents pushed back, but not hard enough. The literal translation of Samson's words read, "She is right in my eyes." In other words, Samson was focused only on the woman's beauty; he had no consideration for her character.

His parents did not know that this was from the Lord, who was seeking an occasion to confront the Philistines; for at that time they were ruling over Israel. (Judges 14:4)

Throughout Samson's story, we learn a comforting truth: our sin will never screw up God's plan. God is a big boy. He's powerful, and he won't be stopped. But this truth comes with an unnerving side as well: we can still screw up our entire lives with our sin. God will accomplish his goals despite our sin… we will simply live tragic lives in the midst of his accomplishments. Samson is the perfect example of someone who accomplished God's goals while living a tragic life.

(5) Samson went down to Timnah together with his father and mother. As they approached the vineyards of Timnah, suddenly a young lion came roaring toward him. (6) The Spirit of the Lord came upon him in power so that he tore the lion apart with his bare hands as he might have torn a young goat. But he told neither his father nor his mother what he had done. (7) Then he went down and talked with the woman, and he liked her.
(8) Some time later, when he went back to marry her, he turned aside to look at the lion's carcass. In it was a swarm of bees and some honey, (9) which he scooped out with his hands and ate as he went along. When he rejoined his parents, he gave them some, and they too ate it. But he did not tell them that he had taken the honey from the lion's carcass. (Judges 14:5-9)

Killing the lion with his bare hands was the first of several amazing feats Samson executed in his life, and a key phrase occurs during every feat: *The Spirit of the Lord came upon him in power.* This phrase reminds us of the simple truth that Samson's power came from God and God only.[2]

The killing of the lion displayed Samson's incredible, God-given strength, but there was also something more subtle being displayed in that moment. Nazirites were not only supposed to abstain from alcohol, but they were supposed to avoid grapes, raisins, and vineyards. Nazirites also weren't supposed to come in contact with anything dead. By walking through a vineyard and later scooping honey out of the body of a dead lion, Samson showed complete disregard for his nazirite vows. In that moment, a steady theme in Samson's life began to emerge: he was reckless, careless, and selfish. He didn't want to play by any rules.

(10) Now his father went down to see the woman. And Samson made a feast there, as was customary for bridegrooms. (11) When he appeared, he was given thirty companions.
(12) "Let me tell you a riddle," Samson said to them. **"If you can give me the answer within the seven days of the feast, I will give you thirty linen garments and thirty sets of clothes. (13) If you can't tell me the answer, you must give me thirty linen garments and thirty sets of clothes."**
"Tell us your riddle," they said. "Let's hear it."
(14) He replied,

> "Out of the eater, something to eat;
> out of the strong, something sweet."

For three days they could not give the answer.
(15) On the fourth day, they said to Samson's wife, "Coax your husband into explaining the riddle for us, or we will burn you and your father's household to death. Did you invite us here to rob us?"
(16) Then Samson's wife threw herself on him, sobbing, "You hate me! You don't really love me. You've given my people a riddle, but you haven't told me the answer."
"I haven't even explained it to my father or mother," he replied, "so why should I explain it to you?" **(17) She cried the whole seven days of the feast. So on the seventh day he finally told her, because she continued to press him. She in turn explained the riddle to her people.**
(18) Before sunset on the seventh day the men of the town said to him,

> "What is sweeter than honey?
> What is stronger than a lion?"
>
> Samson said to them,
>
> "If you had not plowed with my heifer,
> you would not have solved my riddle."
> (Judges 14:10-18)

Wow. Guys, I wouldn't ever use the phrase, *plowing my heifer*, in reference to your wives. Bad idea.

The wedding got kind of weird. Samson wanted to exchange riddles, Samson's groomsmen threatened to murder his wife, and Samson's wife spent the entire seven days of her honeymoon sobbing. Once again, the reckless theme of Samson's life was being highlighted through that moment. He was strong, but unwise – a deadly combination. Look at his response to the whole riddle fiasco:

> **(19) Then the Spirit of the Lord came upon him in power. He went down to Ashkelon, struck down thirty of their men, stripped them of their belongings and gave their clothes to those who had explained the riddle. Burning with anger, he went up to his father's house. (20) And Samson's wife was given to the friend who had attended him at his wedding. (Judges 14:19-20)**

There's that phrase again: *The Spirit of the Lord came upon him in power.* Samson didn't hold up his end of the deal by paying up for losing the riddle. Instead, he attacked a Philistine outpost, killed thirty men, and used their clothing as payment. Samson's purpose was to deliver his people from the Philistine oppression, but he was more focused on petty, personal revenge. This selfishness only intensifies as the story continues.

(1) Later on, at the time of wheat harvest, Samson took a young goat and went to visit his wife. He said, "I'm going to my wife's room." But her father would not let him go in.

(2) "I was so sure you thoroughly hated her," he said, "that I gave her to your friend. Isn't her younger sister more attractive? Take her instead."

(3) Samson said to them, "This time I have a right to get even with the Philistines; I will really harm them." **(4)** So he went out and caught three hundred foxes and tied them tail to tail in pairs. He then fastened a torch to every pair of tails, **(5)** lit the torches and let the foxes loose in the standing grain of the Philistines. He burned up the shocks and standing grain, together with the vineyards and olive groves.

(6) When the Philistines asked, "Who did this?" they were told, "Samson, the Timnite's son-in-law, because his wife was given to his friend."

So the Philistines went up and burned her and her father to death. **(7)** Samson said to them, "Since you've acted like this, I won't stop until I get my revenge on you." **(8)** He attacked them viciously and slaughtered many of them. Then he went down and stayed in a cave in the rock of Etam. (Judges 15:1-8)

The carnage continued to rack up, and it all began with an unwise decision to marry the wrong person.[3] The fallout of Samson's terrible decisions now included the lives of his wife and father-in-law (I guess it also included the lives of three hundred foxes, which I think is awesome… PETA probably disapproves, though). But Samson didn't care. He was bloodthirsty.

Samson's bloodthirstiness also clouded his judgment. When he set fire to the Philistine's fields, he was not only bringing a big blow to their economy, but he was also intentionally making fun of their false god, Dagon, who was the god of grain. He was picking a huge fight.

>   (9) The Philistines went up and camped in Judah, spreading out near Lehi. (10) The men of Judah asked, "Why have you come to fight us?"
>   "We have come to take Samson prisoner," they answered, "to do to him as he did to us."
>   (11) Then three thousand men from Judah went down to the cave in the rock of Etam and said to Samson, "Don't you realize that the Philistines are rulers over us? What have you done to us?"
>   He answered, "I merely did to them what they did to me."
>   (12) They said to him, "We've come to tie you up and hand you over to the Philistines."
>   Samson said, "Swear to me that you won't kill me yourselves."
>   (13) "Agreed," they answered. "We will only tie you up and hand you over to them. We will not kill you." So they bound him with two new ropes and led him up from the rock. (Judges 15:9-13)

An old Puritan writer, Thomas Brooks, claimed that men's offenses are increased by their obligations.[4] Someone you might be more familiar with, Spiderman, said it this way: *With great power comes great responsibility.* Jesus, the guy who matters the most, said it this way: *To whom much has been given, much is required.*[5]

Here's what I mean. Everyone loves the walk-on who gets a chance to play and squeezes the most out of his limited talent, but nobody loves the number one draft pick who blows his chance. No one respects the man who squanders his talents and wastes his gifts.

Samson had been given a lot, but he wasted it all. He might have been strong, but he was a terrible leader. He might have had power, but he was reckless with that power and hurt a lot of people. The vicious cycle of revenge was all Samson could focus on. He was too concerned with himself to lead his own people. In turn, his people had no interest in following or dying under his leadership.

(14) As he approached Lehi, the Philistines came toward him shouting. The Spirit of the Lord came upon him in power. The ropes on his arms became like charred flax, and the bindings dropped from his hands. (15) Finding a fresh jawbone of a donkey, he grabbed it and struck down a thousand men.
(16) Then Samson said,

> **"With a donkey's jawbone**
> **I have made donkeys of them.**
> **With a donkey's jawbone**
> **I have killed a thousand men."**
> **(Judges 15:14-16)**

The Spirit of the Lord came upon him in power. Once again, even though he had no interest in God's desires, Samson was accomplishing God's purposes in regard to delivering the Israelites from Philistine oppression.

(18) Because he was very thirsty, he cried out to the Lord, "You have given your servant this great victory. Must I now die of thirst and fall into the hands of the uncircumcised?" (19) Then God opened up the hollow place in Lehi, and water came out of it. When Samson drank, his strength returned and he revived. (Judges 15:18-19a)

The story of Samson is tricky because, despite the reckless disregard for his vows and his people, Samson often remembered where his strength came from: *You have given me this great victory.* When Samson looked in the mirror, he recognized that his strength came from God. The story is also tricky because, even in the middle of the mess of a life that Samson had created, God continued to provide for him. I am always amazed with God's patience with people like Samson… with people like me… with people like us.

But Samson's total disregard for anyone or anything other than himself continued:

(1) One day Samson went to Gaza, where he saw a prostitute. He went in to spend the night with her. (2) The people of Gaza were told, "Samson is here!" So they surrounded the place and lay in wait for him all night at the city gate. They made no move during the night, saying, "At dawn we'll kill him."
(3) But Samson lay there only until the middle of the night. Then he got up and took hold of the doors of the city gate, together with the two posts, and tore them loose, bar and all. He lifted them to his shoulders and carried them to the top of the hill that faces Hebron.
(Judges 16:1-3)

I would argue that Samson was a sex addict. He objectified women at every opportunity, and he showed significant weakness by visiting prostitutes. A subtle clue in the scripture suggests that Samson's arrogance would soon catch up to him: when Samson busted up the town gate – a gate that archaeologists estimate to have weighed nearly 5,000 pounds – and carried it up a hill for two miles, there is no mention of the Spirit of the Lord. None. Tragedy is just around the corner.

I wish that didn't describe some of us reading this book, but the truth is that many of us, especially some of us men, have gotten away with a lot. We haven't had any major consequences for our recklessness, so we think very highly of ourselves. We think we are strong and indestructible. We think we can run over anyone and anything that stands in our way, and we think this ability to dominate is what makes us men. We aren't interested in anyone speaking truth into our lives because we think we can do it alone. To quote a good friend of mine: *Being alone doesn't make you a man… it just makes you alone.*

That is the truth. Some of us have become so focused on our own strength that we have become blind to our own weaknesses. A real man acknowledges his weaknesses and attacks them. The only other alternative is to continue pretending we don't have any. Do you know what I call someone who pretends they are indestructible? *A little boy.* Seriously. My four-year-old son does that. Whenever he puts on his Iron Man costume with the cool mask and fake muscles, he thinks he can jump off of anything, pick up anything, and fight anyone. It's really kind of funny… because he's four. But when you become an adult, that joke isn't funny anymore. When you are forty-four, and you're still hiding behind your muscles, it's just sad.

Like Samson, if you don't wake up and quit pretending that you can rely on your own strength, tragedy is right around the corner.

(4) Some time later, he fell in love with a woman in the Valley of Sorek whose name was Delilah. (5) The rulers of the Philistines went to her and said, "See if you can lure him into showing you the secret of his great strength and how we can overpower him so we may tie him up and subdue him. Each one of us will give you eleven hundred shekels of silver."
(6) So Delilah said to Samson, "Tell me the secret of your great strength and how you can be tied up and subdued."

(7) Samson answered her, "If anyone ties me with seven fresh thongs that have not been dried, I'll become as weak as any other man." (Judges 16:4-7)

Once again, Samson displayed a weakness for women. The text doesn't explicitly say that Delilah was a Philistine woman, but that *is* the contextual implication. Don't you think that Samson should have learned his lesson by now?

Here's the most interesting aspect of this part of Samson's story: the Philistines didn't want to kill him anymore. Instead, they wanted to subdue him. They believed they could change Samson's alliances and use him for their own benefit. Now, why would they have thought that? Because… over the years, the Philistines had noticed something about Samson: he had no character, loyalty, or discipline.

There is a truth that comes screaming off of these pages: you can only pretend for so long. For a while, everyone believed that Samson was a pious, noble, loyal, diligent, self-controlled Nazirite, but eventually, they found him out. You can pretend for a while, but your true character will eventually betray you, and when your true character is unveiled, your enemies will capitalize on your weaknesses. They will destroy you.

Samson's true character began to betray him, and because he believed he could do whatever he wanted, he got really risky:

(8) Then the rulers of the Philistines brought her seven fresh thongs that had not been dried, and she tied him with them. (9) With men hidden in the room, she called to him, "Samson, the Philistines are upon you!" But he snapped the thongs as easily as a piece of string snaps

when it comes close to a flame. So the secret of his strength was not discovered.

(10) Then Delilah said to Samson, "You have made a fool of me; you lied to me. Come now, tell me how you can be tied."

(11) He said, "If anyone ties me securely with new ropes that have never been used, I'll become as weak as any other man."

(12) So Delilah took new ropes and tied him with them. Then, with men hidden in the room, she called to him, "Samson, the Philistines are upon you!" But he snapped the ropes off his arms as if they were threads.

(13) Delilah then said to Samson, "Until now, you have been making a fool of me and lying to me. Tell me how you can be tied."

He replied, "If you weave the seven braids of my head into the fabric on the loom and tighten it with the pin, I'll become as weak as any other man." So while he was sleeping, Delilah took the seven braids of his head, wove them into the fabric (14) and tightened it with the pin.

Again she called to him, "Samson, the Philistines are upon you!" He awoke from his sleep and pulled up the pin and the loom, with the fabric.

(15) Then she said to him, "How can you say, 'I love you,' when you won't confide in me? This is the third time you have made a fool of me and haven't told me the secret of your great strength." (16) With such nagging she prodded him day after day until he was tired to death.

(17) So he told her everything. "No razor has ever been used on my head," he said, "because I have been a Nazirite set apart to God from birth. If my head were shaved, my strength would leave me, and I would become as weak as any other man."

(18) When Delilah saw that he had told her everything, she sent word to the rulers of the Philistines, "Come back once more; he has told me everything." So the rulers

of the Philistines returned with the silver in their hands. (19) Having put him to sleep on her lap, she called a man to shave off the seven braids of his hair, and so began to subdue him. And his strength left him.

(20) Then she called, "Samson, the Philistines are upon you!"

He awoke from his sleep and thought, "I'll go out as before and shake myself free." But he did not know that the Lord had left him.

(21) Then the Philistines seized him, gouged out his eyes and took him down to Gaza. Binding him with bronze shackles, they set him to grinding in the prison. (Judges 16:8-21)

His hair was the only component of the nazirite vow that Samson had not already violated, but his power had nothing to do with his hair. His power came from God.

When babies are learning to walk, you can stand behind them, hold their hands, and they'll walk fairly well, but the second you let go, they'll fall down. Eventually, babies will become overly confident and try to let go of your hands. They might get one or two steps, but they inevitably sway, totter, and pitch toward the ground. This is the same picture we see with Samson and Delilah. Samson was the overconfident child who chose to let go of his father's hands. He was the child who had forgotten where his strength came from.

God allowed everything to come crashing down around Samson. This was God's way of graciously saying to Samson, *Enough is enough. You think you're indestructible, but I have to show you that you aren't. You've lost your way. You've violated every commitment you ever made, you've run over everyone in your life, and the trail of bodies in your wake is too many to count. As painful as this will be, I have to remind you where your strength comes from. It's time to remember that you aren't God... I AM.*

Have you ever been in that place? It's not a fun place, but it's sometimes the most gracious place God can provide for us. Some people call it 'rock bottom', and some call it 'the end of the rope'. It's the place where you finally come to your senses.

What will it take for *you* to come to your senses?

Samson found himself blind, which is ironic because it was his eyes that got him in the most trouble. He found himself grinding grain in prison. Grinding was the work of a slave, but Samson was already familiar with slavery. He had been a slave to his own reckless impulses long before he was ever a slave to the Philistines.

Do you ever feel like a slave to your own destructive behavior?

(23) Now the rulers of the Philistines assembled to offer a great sacrifice to Dagon their god and to celebrate, saying, "Our god has delivered Samson, our enemy, into our hands."
(24) When the people saw him, they praised their god, saying,

> **"Our god has delivered our enemy**
> **into our hands,**
> **the one who laid waste our land**
> **and multiplied our slain."**

(25) While they were in high spirits, they shouted, "Bring out Samson to entertain us." So they called Samson out of the prison, and he performed for them.
When they stood him among the pillars, (26) Samson

said to the servant who held his hand, "Put me where I can feel the pillars that support the temple, so that I may lean against them." (27) Now the temple was crowded with men and women; all the rulers of the Philistines were there, and on the roof were about three thousand men and women watching Samson perform. (28) Then Samson prayed to the Lord, "O Sovereign Lord, remember me. O God, please strengthen me just once more, and let me with one blow get revenge on the Philistines for my two eyes." (29) Then Samson reached toward the two central pillars on which the temple stood. Bracing himself against them, his right hand on the one and his left hand on the other, (30) Samson said, "Let me die with the Philistines!" Then he pushed with all his might, and down came the temple on the rulers and all the people in it. Thus he killed many more when he died than while he lived.
 (Judges 16:23-30)

I don't think that Samson ever 'got it'. Even at the end of his life, he was most focused on revenge for the gouging of his eyes. Did he defeat the Philistines? Yes, but his motivations were always selfish. While God accomplished his goals despite Samson's reckless behavior, Samson still lived an awful life. He failed to combine strength with wisdom:

A wise man is full of strength, and a man of knowledge enhances his might. (Proverbs 24:5 ESV)

Wisdom must come before strength, and knowledge must come before might. Samson was strong, but he was *not* wise, and that's a deadly combination.

Vinnie – Strength with wisdom

When it comes to strength and wisdom, I think there's a lot we can learn about what *not* to do from a guy named

Samson, and there's a lot we can learn about what *to* do from a guy named Vinnie Lopez. What follows is the transcription of a video interview I held with Vinnie in September of 2010:

> SCOTT: *Vinnie, tell us a little bit about how long you've been into mixed martial arts. What do you love about it? Why do you do it?*
>
> VINNIE: I've officially been doing mixed martial arts since 2003, but I didn't really get serious about it until 2008. Basically, it has been a life-changer for me. The discipline and the focus that it requires have branched off into every other part of my life. From the combination of a couple of things, I've become a better father, a better son, a better brother, and a better person in general, and one of those things is definitely the training.
>
> SCOTT: *When you say that you've become a better father, son, and brother through fighting, I'm sure that confuses most people, so explain that a little bit.*
>
> VINNIE: Fighting has given me direction. It has given me focus. It requires so much discipline, and it leaves little room for error. You can't be partying. You can't be drinking. You know that you have to wake up the next day and train with some of the best in the world. That kind of discipline just made me a better person… that and staying in the Word a little bit more, of course.
>
> SCOTT: *Very cool. When you meet people in passing,*

and they ask what you do, how do they react to hearing that you are an MMA fighter?

VINNIE: It's anywhere from admiration to, *You do what?* A lot of people don't understand. A lot of people think that this is just a 'tough guy' sport. They almost anticipate you to be this super aggressive person with no control, but it's almost the exact opposite. You have to have total control of yourself. You have to have total patience.

SCOTT: *You're not only a fighter, but you're also a father. Talk about that for a bit.*

VINNIE: My kids are my life. I wake up every day so lucky to have two beautiful children. My son is thirteen. We do a lot of stuff together. He's really into sports and football. He's a fighter, too – he's pretty good. My daughter is five... I just got done going through a fight for her, actually. I battled for her, I won, and now we're having a great time together. We have a great relationship, and we're getting to know each other that much more. It's the best part of my life, being a father. It *is* my life.

SCOTT: *Awesome. If you could pick a few words that you wish described who you are, what would they be? Even if you're thinking, "I don't know if they describe me perfectly right now," none of us are perfectly who we want to be. So if you had to pick a few words to describe Vinnie Lopez, what would you say?*

VINNIE: 'Diligent'. I train hard. I work hard. I'm loyal. Once you become my friend, you're my friend for life – there's no faltering from that. And 'loving'. I love my family immensely. My children are the light of my life.[6]

From the outside, there are a lot of preconceived notions that people might have about a guy like Vinnie: *Look at that dude! He's a fighter. He has lots of tattoos. I'll bet he's mean. I'll bet he's crazy, he lacks self-control, and he's reckless.*

This actually used to be the case with Vinnie, but as you can tell from that interview, Vinnie woke up. Vinnie began paying attention. He no longer lives under the illusion that he is indestructible. He is learning that he can't use his strength to do whatever he wants. He is learning about strength under control.

Do you know what that's called? It's called *wisdom*. When you combine strength and wisdom, they become a powerful combination. When you put those two things together, a man can do a lot of amazing things.

When you put those two together, you can be a better dad to your children.

When you put those two together, you can actually control yourself rather than fly off the handle and run people over.

When you put those two together, you can be a credible leader whom people want to follow.

When you put those two together, you are on your way to becoming a man... a *real* man.

When you put strength and wisdom together, you start to look like Jesus.

Jesus had both strength *and* wisdom. There has never been a stronger man on the face of this planet. Even though he was always the most powerful man in every room he ever stood in, Jesus never used his strength to run people over, bully people, or push people around. Instead, he used his strength to serve, teach, lead, and heal. Ultimately, he used his strength to get crucified.

This doesn't mean that Jesus never got angry; he just got angry in the right situations because there *is* such a thing as righteous anger. When Jesus watched people get run over, he became angry. When followers of God disregarded poor, mistreated women and children, he became angry. He became *really* angry when religious people trivialized worship by standing between God and the people God loves. Those were the times when Jesus ran into temples, threw tables over, and chased people out – one time, with a whip. Jesus was not (and is not) a weakling. He's the most real man to have ever walked the face of this earth. There is a time and a place to show your strength, but wisdom must be guiding that strength.

We probably need to broaden the definition of strength. Yes… a wise and knowledgeable man will take care of his body and stay strong. You cannot biblically make a case for letting your body go, eating terribly, and becoming lazy. But strength is so much bigger than that…

I've seen Vinnie train. I've seen Vinnie fight. I will attend more of his fights, but his fighting is not the best display of his strength. Not by a long shot.

When Vinnie takes his five-year-old daughter out on 'daddy-dates'… *that* is strength.

When Vinnie goes to every one of his thirteen-year-old son's football games... *that* is strength.

When Vinnie shows up to Flatirons, week after week, to learn more about Jesus and how the Bible applies to his life... *that* is strength.

Vinnie once said something really cool to me: *There are two things that are primarily responsible for turning my life around: Flatirons and Fighting.*

I think that's awesome. You see... Vinnie would be the first to tell you that he's far from perfect. Vinnie is a work in progress just like the rest of us, but unlike Samson, Vinnie is taking his strength and combining it with wisdom.

Samson is mentioned only one more time in the Bible. In the New Testament, he is among many in a list of people who had great faith.[7] In other words, Samson's problem wasn't faith; he knew that his strength came from God. Samson's problem was that he squandered that gift. Sure... Samson is in heaven, but he still lived a horrible life. It is more than possible to live a terrible, train wreck of a life and *still* get into heaven, but is that really what you want?

Be wise. Stop relying on your own strength, and begin relying on someone greater, stronger, bigger, and wiser than you. You are God's child, and as long as you stay connected to him, you will be strong. The moment you let go of your father is the moment you become weak. Some of you may be thinking, *No, no, no. If I have to hold on to God to be strong, then I'm actually weak.*

Listen to what Paul said: **For when I am weak, then I am strong. (2 Corinthians 12:10b)**

When we live our lives with wisdom… when we rely on God and live our lives connected to him… when we quit relying on our own strength and begin recognizing our weaknesses… then, in an ironic twist, we become strong. We become strong only because God is strong in us and through us.

1. The entire story of Samson can be found in Judges 13-16.

2. Growing up, whenever I pictured Samson, I always imagined a 'Schwarzenegger' type of man – someone massive and intimidating. However, there is no description of Samson's physical appearance in the Bible. I can't help but think that, in order to further demonstrate the power of God, Samson probably looked more like Barney Fife. I'll bet there was no one more shocked at Samson's strength than Samson himself.

3. See **Appendix: A note on marriage** for the marital applications found in Samson's story.

4. A truth repeatedly taught in Thomas Brooks' book entitled *Precious Remedies Against Satan's Devices*.

5. Luke 12:48.

6. My video interview with Vinnie is available for viewing under the "Resources: Listen/Watch Messages" tab at www.flatironschurch.com. Watch Week Three of *Grow A Pair* (September 25-26, 2010).

7. Hebrews 11:32-34.

03. Samson and Vinnie... Strength and Wisdom General Discussion Questions

Core:

1. What was your familiarity with the Samson story before reading this chapter? What was new to you about the life and struggles of Samson?

2. Samson looked outwardly honorable, but on the inside, his character was corrupt. He used his strength in ways that God never intended, and it ruined his life. Can you relate to Samson's dual nature in any way?

3. Samson was reckless, careless, and selfish. How do you see this demonstrated in Samson's life, and what were the consequences for his actions?

4. You can pretend for a while, but your true character will eventually betray you. Do you believe this? If so, what does this betrayal of true character look like?

5. Is there a way to come to your senses before hitting rock bottom? If so, how?

6. Regardless of Samson's wisdom and intentions, God accomplished his purposes through Samson. However, do you think that Samson ever 'got it'?

7. If wisdom is strength under control, then how did Jesus model wisdom better than anyone else in history?

8. Are there any areas of your life in which you need to stop relying on your own strength and begin relying on God?

Challenge:

1. Memorize Proverbs 24:5: **A wise man is full of strength, and a man of knowledge enhances his might.**

2. Write down an area in your life in which you want to develop better character by growing in wisdom. Ask God to produce this strength, wisdom, and character in your life.

03. Samson and Vinnie... Strength and Wisdom Discussion Questions for Women

Core:

1. When you think of a strong man, who is the first person to come to mind?

2. Would you describe Samson as a strong man?

3. In your opinion, what was Samson's greatest failure?

4. How would you describe Samson's view of women? What were his standards for women?

5. Read Proverbs 31:10-31. Discuss the traits that God says make a good wife.

6. Who would you say is the strongest woman you know?

7. Is strength a characteristic that God desires to see in women? Is strength displayed differently in women than in men?

8. Do you view any of the traits we've discussed thus far – identity, integrity, strength, and wisdom – as particularly masculine or feminine? Why?

9. Look again at Proverbs 31, specifically verses 25, 26, and 30. What is the key to a woman's wisdom?

10. What are your thoughts about Vinnie's story?

11. Samson didn't believe that he had to play by the rules. Have you ever known a man or woman who has refused to play by the rules?

12. How might Samson's story have been different if the desire of his heart had been to chase after God in every decision?

Challenge:

1. Think about the teachings Samson's story contains about healthy relationships between men and women.

2. This week, make an effort to know your weaknesses, and ask God to direct you in addressing them.

04.
David, Part One... Humility

By
Jim Burgen

04.
David, Part One… Humility

> **The Lord does not look at the things man looks at. Man looks at the outward appearance, but the Lord looks at the heart. (1 Samuel 16:7b)**

This statement occurred during an argument with God (here is some quick advice: don't ever argue with God because it's never a good idea… I promise you will lose). God had chosen a skinny, teenage boy named David to be the next king of Israel, and David's father, Jesse, was arguing with God about this decision. Jesse's argument sounded like this: *God, are you serious? You want David to be the next king? Please, look at all of my other sons. They are bigger, stronger, faster, and much more qualified to be king. My other sons are perfect candidates, but you want to choose my little shepherd boy? Why?*

God responded, *If I were only counting on the outward appearances and physical qualities of your sons, then you'd be absolutely correct, but those qualities aren't important to me. David has something special going on inside his heart – something that makes him worthy to be the king of Israel.*

God obviously thought highly of David's character. In fact, the first reference to David in the Bible is one of the most flattering descriptions of a man's character that I've ever read. God himself gave the description when he decided to fire the first king of Israel, Saul. God explained to Saul why he was being fired and described the character of the new, future king:

But now your kingdom will not endure; the Lord has sought out a man after his own heart and appointed him leader of his people, because you have not kept the Lord's command. (1 Samuel 13:14)

A man after God's own heart…

I would be thrilled if God described me as 'a man after his own heart'. Can you imagine? *Hey angels… come over here a second. You see Jim down there? That's what I'm talking about! Not only is he funny, charming, and good-looking* (okay… maybe I'm going overboard)*, but he's also a man after my own heart. That's what it looks like to believe in my promises. That's what it looks like to chase after my heart.*

Don't you desire that same description? *You are a man after God's own heart. You are a woman after God's own heart.*

What does it take to be described by God in such a wonderful way?

As we've already discovered, God does not judge a person on his or her outward appearances or circumstances. In fact, God says that even the mistakes we've made and the messes we've survived don't factor into his evaluations of our character. Don't get me wrong… he deeply cares about our pasts because he deeply cares about *us*, but at the same time, our pasts no longer define our futures.

Also, as we're about to learn through the story of David, making mistakes does not disqualify us from being men and women after God's own heart. We will be held accountable for our mistakes, and those failures might even create disastrous consequences for our lives, but if we hold onto certain pairs of crucial characteristics, then we still have a shot at being true men and women of God.

We've already learned about *identity* and *integrity*, as well as *strength* and *wisdom*. In the next two chapters, using the story of David as an example, we will learn about another essential pair that has gone missing in our lives. [1]

A man after God's own heart

God picked David to be the next king of Israel when David was between the ages of thirteen and seventeen [2], so rather than being told to immediately ascend to the throne, David was commanded to continue tending to his sheep. Meanwhile, David's brothers left home to join the Israelites in a battle against the Philistines (yes, the same people group who occupied Israel during Samson's time).

One day, Jesse sent David to the battlefield in order to take his brothers some food. When David arrived, he found the two armies separated by a valley and all of the Israelite soldiers hiding from the Philistines. David soon learned that the Israelite army was terrified of a Philistine warrior named Goliath. I'm sure you've all heard about Goliath, but he wasn't a giant – this isn't a fairy tale. Goliath was simply *huge*. He was nearly nine feet tall, he carried a massive sword and shield, and he was a proven champion on the battlefield. Everyday, Goliath would walk down into the dividing valley and yell to the Israelites, *Send your toughest warrior down into this valley to fight a one-on-one battle with me. Winner takes all! If your warrior wins, then the Philistines will be your slaves. If I win, then your people will be the Philistines' slaves.*

Until David showed up, none of the Israelite warriors were willing to fight Goliath. David examined the situation, peered across the valley at Goliath, and proclaimed in his squeaky, undeveloped, teenage voice, *I'll do it!*

Of course, the Israelites responded with shocked disbelief. *You can't do that! You're just a punk boy! And Goliath… Goliath is a man… a huge, towering, mighty warrior of a man. You're out of your league. You're in over your head. Who do you think you are?*

But David didn't budge:

(33) Saul replied, "You are not able to go out against this Philistine and fight him; you are only a boy, and he has been a fighting man from his youth."
(34) But David said to Saul, "Your servant has been keeping his father's sheep. When a lion or a bear came and carried off a sheep from the flock, (35) I went after it, struck it and rescued the sheep from its mouth. When it turned on me, I seized it by its hair, struck it and killed it. (36) Your servant has killed both the lion and the bear; this uncircumcised Philistine will be like one of them, because he has defied the armies of the living God. (37) The Lord who delivered me from the paw of the lion and the paw of the bear will deliver me from the hand of this Philistine."
Saul said to David, "Go, and the Lord be with you." (1 Samuel 17:33-37)

David's response to Saul reveals four aspects of his character that will sound very familiar. First, David was incredibly clear about his identity. He knew God's character, and he knew his place before God. Second, because of his sense of identity, David was willing to march into action. He lived and acted out of his identity; in other words, he was a man of integrity. Third, David was strong. I'm not talking about physical strength – he was only a boy. Instead, I'm talking about the kind of strength that can only come through God. David didn't take credit for slaying the bear or lion, and he didn't take credit for proclaiming the death of Goliath. He knew that God deserved that credit. Lastly, David was wise. David saw what everybody else was missing: God was offering the Israelites a chance to prove his own greatness through the slaying of Goliath.

A man after God's own heart…

Now, whether you've spent time in church or not, you most likely know the end of the David and Goliath story. David, the skinny, teenage shepherd, will eventually walk down into the valley, look Goliath in the eye, and say, *God is going to help me strike you down and cut your head off.*

Goliath will laugh at David. *I'd like to see you try!*

Then, David will strike Goliath down and cut his head off. It's an awesome story. You should read it sometime. The rest of 1 Samuel is about how David became a great warrior and leader. After his battle against Goliath, Saul hired David to work for the country. Eventually, Saul died, and David rose to the throne.

Similar to every other story we've told throughout this book, I truly wish the story of David ended here: *…and he lived happily ever after!* However, as we've already discussed, I don't want to write about the sanitized, Sunday school versions of these Bible stories. I want to write about the truth. And the truth is that David's life got really messy after Goliath. Sure, he may have been a real man – he possessed identity, integrity, strength, and wisdom – but he was also a *human*. And humans make mistakes, don't we?

We can love God, love our family, love our friends, go to church every weekend, drink communion, and get baptized two or three times... but we still have the ability to totally mess our lives over. This is simply part of being human, and in this way, David is *definitely* our king.

A human after God's own heart

I want to look at an event that occurred later in David's life that exemplifies David's humanness.[3] One night, after David had become king, he walked onto the roof of his palace to cool off because he was having trouble sleeping. If you already know this story, then you know that he didn't cool off at all... he actually began to heat up. From the palace roof, David could see into the neighbor's window. In that window, David saw a beautiful, naked woman taking a bath. Let me correct that: David saw a beautiful, naked, *married* woman taking a bath. This woman's name was Bathsheba.

How do you think David – the strong and wise man of integrity... the man after God's own heart... the very *married* man after God's own heart – reacted in this situation?

He made a *huge* mistake because he was human.

Beginning with this moment on the roof, over the next few weeks of his life, David will forget the identity that God had given him: *I don't care who you are... I don't care who I am... I just want to have sex with Bathsheba.* David will show no respect or care for Bathsheba, he will become a total liar (the opposite of integrity, by the way), and he will abuse the power of his kingship. Remember... this is still David, the man after God's own heart.

After seeing Bathsheba from his roof, David immediately sent for her and slept with her. That seems bad enough, but it gets worse. The only reason Bathsheba could leave her house without raising any suspicion from her husband was because her husband, Uriah, was off at war… fighting for David! Bathsheba became pregnant with David's child, and David realized he needed to cover his mess up quickly, so he brought Uriah home from battle, had dinner with him, and said, *Uriah! You're such a good soldier and husband. Go! Enjoy your time home and sleep with your wife!*

David was hoping that, if no one did the math, he would get away with impregnating Bathsheba. But David didn't count on Uriah being a man of integrity. Uriah said to David, *All of my buddies are still at war, and they don't get to come home to sleep with their wives. Therefore, I won't sleep with mine* (I kind of think Uriah is crazy for that… but whatever). The next night, David threw a huge party to get Uriah drunk. David hoped Uriah would sleep with Bathsheba if he was drunk, but Uriah merely passed out in his own front yard.

David was running out of options, so he turned to Plan B.

David sent Uriah back to the war with a sealed message for the general. The message read: *Send Uriah to the most dangerous frontlines. When the battle gets intense, pull everyone back but Uriah… let him die.*

Plan B worked.

David successfully murdered Uriah, married Uriah's grieving widow, and grinned at his own clever plan. *I got away with it! No one will ever know!*

But David didn't get away with his murder. Why? You probably won't like this answer – in fact, I hate giving this answer – but too bad. David didn't get away with his sin because *God loved him*. The worst thing God could have done for David would have been to act like David's sin didn't matter. The most hateful, unloving thing God could have said to David would have been, *Let's just forget about this and move on. Let's pretend like this never happened.*

Instead, God sent David a prophet named Nathan. Nathan asked David if he wanted to hear a story. I'll bet that David was excited about storytelling time. He was, after all, a poet. I'll bet he replied to Nathan, *Sure! You tell me a story, I'll tell you a story, we'll roast some S'mores, and we'll make a night of it!* But David wasn't expecting the kind of story Nathan had to tell:

(1) The Lord sent Nathan to David. When he came to him, he said, "There were two men in a certain town, one rich and the other poor. (2) The rich man had a very large number of sheep and cattle, (3) but the poor man had nothing except one little ewe lamb he had bought. He raised it, and it grew up with him and his children. It shared his food, drank from his cup and even slept in his arms. It was like a daughter to him.
(4) "Now a traveler came to the rich man, but the rich man refrained from taking one of his own sheep or cattle to prepare a meal for the traveler who had come to him. Instead, he took the ewe lamb that belonged to the poor man and prepared it for the one who had come to him." (2 Samuel 12:1-4)

At this point in the story, David had had enough. This wasn't a fantasy story anymore, and he was furious. David used to be a shepherd. He knew what it was like to love your flock, and he knew how terrible it was for a man to steal another man's sheep. David exploded on Nathan:

(5) David burned with anger against the man and said to Nathan, "As surely as the Lord lives, the man who

did this deserves to die! (6) He must pay for that lamb four times over, because he did such a thing and had no pity."

(7) Then Nathan said to David, "You are the man! This is what the Lord, the God of Israel, says: 'I anointed you king over Israel, and I delivered you from the hand of Saul. (8) I gave your master's house to you, and your master's wives into your arms. I gave you the house of Israel and Judah. And if all this had been too little, I would have given you even more. (9) Why did you despise the word of the Lord by doing what is evil in his eyes? You struck down Uriah the Hittite with the sword and took his wife to be your own. You killed him with the sword of the Ammonites. (10) Now, therefore, the sword will never depart from your house, because you despised me and took the wife of Uriah the Hittite to be your own.'

(11) "This is what the Lord says: 'Out of your own household I am going to bring calamity upon you. Before your very eyes I will take your wives and give them to one who is close to you, and he will lie with your wives in broad daylight. (12) You did it in secret, but I will do this thing in broad daylight before all Israel.'" (2 Samuel 12:5-12)

This was an '*Oh Crap!*' moment for David: *So… we were never talking about sheep, were we Nathan?*

The consequences of David's sin were going to be difficult to deal with: *David, you really, really messed up. God handpicked you to lead his nation. He delivered you from all of your enemies. He gave you a palace, servants, and an entire country. He would have given you anything!* <u>You</u> *struck down Uriah. You might as well have taken the sword yourself and pushed it through Uriah's gut. From now on, your life is going to look different. There will be battles fought in your home for the rest of your life. You snuck around in secret, but your own sons will sleep with your wives in broad daylight. Your family will crumble at your feet.*

The consequences of David's sin didn't exist because God wanted to punish him and ruin the rest of his life. There were consequences for David's sin because that is simply how life works. When you make mistakes, life and the people around you will naturally react. Sometimes, those reactions can be devastating.

Look at David's response:

(13)Then David said to Nathan, "I have sinned against the Lord."
Nathan replied, "The Lord has taken away your sin. You are not going to die." (2 Samuel 12:13)

Throughout this book, we've been trying to land on a definition of true manhood. In David's response, we find another characteristic that is missing from many of our lives: *humility*.

You might know your true identity, and you might be living with integrity. You might be strong, and you might be making wise decisions. But what happens when you make a mistake? I don't care how strong, wise, or sure of your identity you are… unless you are Jesus himself, you are going to make mistakes. This isn't a cop out. This doesn't make all of your mistakes permissible. This is simply the truth.

The question is, *How should I act when I make a mistake?*

We find our answer in David. When David was confronted with the truth of his sin, he didn't get defensive: *It's not my fault! Plus, it's not that big of a deal. Some of my friends (not to mention the last king) have done much worse! I'm not the first to make a mistake.*

David didn't try to rationalize his mistakes: *Okay, so I made a sexual mistake… but I'm only a man! I'm human, and I have needs! My marriage is in the tank. I've asked for certain things from my wife, and she always says, "No." So no wonder I had to run to Bathsheba's arms! Who could blame me?*

David doesn't get defensive, and he doesn't rationalize his sin. Instead, he humbly admits his faults: *You're right. I am the man, and I'm responsible. This is my fault. I screwed up. I'm sorry, and I don't want to do this anymore.*

David wrote a lot of Psalms during this time of his life, and in these songs, you will consistently find the following words: *I'm brokenhearted, I'm contrite, I confess, I repent, I've changed my mind.* All of these words have a single, biblical root: *humility.*

Humility

Humility is the first half of the missing pair of characteristics that I want to discuss. *Humility* is not equivalent to *humiliation*; humility is the opposite of arrogance. If you are humble, you don't defend your mistakes or rationalize your poor decisions. You don't blame other people for your decisions. If you are humble, you simply own up to your sins: *I am the man, and this is my fault. I have some reasons for what I did, but none of these reasons are justifiable excuses. I made a choice… I made the wrong choice. This is my fault, so where do I go from here?*

When God saw David, the little shepherd boy, and proclaimed, *You are a man after my own heart*, do you think God knew about David's relationship with Bathsheba and Uriah later down the road? Of course he did! God knows everything. David was not called 'a man after God's own heart' because he never made mistakes. He was called 'a man after God's own heart' because, when he *did* make mistakes, he reacted with humility.

Here is the question I want to ask you, and I want you to continually ask yourself: *Are you humble?*

Go look in the mirror and honestly assess your life. What is your story?

Once upon a time, there was this guy, this girl, this married businessman, this single cop, this career woman, this stay-at-home mom, this college student, or this fifteen-year-old high school kid... and one day, this person...

...knew the right thing to do, but purposely did the opposite.

...was put in a position of trust and power, but abused that position.

...made a promise to a person they loved, and then broke that promise.

...made a decision to follow through with an action that they knew was wrong, but hoped that, with enough time, their mistake wouldn't matter anymore.

...was frustrated with life and secretly made mistakes, but now lives with the fear of being discovered... the fear of having their dirty secrets dragged into the spotlight.

What's your story? Because I'm sure that it probably sounds close to at least one of those stories. David's story is my story – I'm not throwing stones. We've all got the mistake-making part of life down. I'm not asking if you've ever made a

David, Part One… Humility - 95

mistake. You have. I have. David did. Instead, I'm asking if your first reaction to sin is one of humility: *You're right. I'm the man. I'm the woman. I'm responsible. This is my fault.*

Does humility even fall into your first fifty responses? I know that I go through just about every other response in the book before I respond to my sin with humility. I try to defend my mistakes. I try to minimize my sins. I try to rationalize my decisions or blame others for my choices. I try to point toward people who have made bigger mistakes. I get angry with God for bringing my secrets out into the open. Sometimes, I even use the phrase, *God, why are you doing this to me?*

Let me clear something up. God didn't do this to you. You did this to yourself. Actually, let me adjust that statement: if God is doing *anything* to you, he is showing you love because he still considers you his child:

(5) And you have forgotten that word of encouragement that addresses you as sons:

**"My son, do not make light of the Lord's discipline,
and do not lose heart when he rebukes you,
(6) because the Lord disciplines those he loves,
and he punishes everyone he accepts as a son.**

(7) Endure hardship as discipline; God is treating you as sons. For what son is not disciplined by his father? (Hebrews 12:5-7)

In other words, God is saying, *I love you. You are my child. When I discipline you, it's not because I hate you or I'm angry with you. I discipline you because I love you. In a way, my discipline is a form of encouragement. I want you to quit making poor decisions only because I love you as my own child, and you cannot go on living like this.*

God disciplines his children out of love. In fact, if God is not disciplining you, then I'd be *more* worried. James, the half-brother of Jesus, said it this way:

But he gives us more grace. That is why Scripture says:

**"God opposes the proud
   but gives grace to the humble." (James 4:6)**

We've been searching for the definition of 'a man after God's own heart'. The definition is *not*, "a man who never makes a stupid, bone-headed mistake." Instead, the definition is, "a man who, after making stupid, bone-headed mistakes, humbly admits to his failures, accepts the blame and consequences, and does everything in his power to get back on course." According to God, a person who lives his or her life by that description is not just a man or woman, but a forgiven son or daughter of God.

With God's grace, we can become *men and women after God's own heart.*

* * * * * *

We can humbly admit to our faults, and we can trust that God will forgive us for anything and everything we could ever screw up, but that doesn't mean there won't be consequences for our terrible decisions. As we will learn in the next chapter, the consequences of David's sin followed him. Even worse, the consequences of David's sin followed his family. The fallout of his mistakes landed on everyone around him, and David's life got incredibly difficult.

    The first half of the missing pair of characteristics that we see illuminated in David's life is *humility*, but until paired with another characteristic, humility will only get us halfway home.

1.   The story of David is quite long, so I'll only be summarizing in this chapter. To read his whole story, check out 1 Samuel 16 through 1 Kings 2.

2.   Young men and women: God is not waiting to pay attention to you. He is not waiting for you to 'grow up'. He is not waiting for you to graduate high school, attend college, land a decent job, or start a family. No … instead, God is paying attention to you at this very moment. He already has a plan for you, and this is a very exciting truth.

3.   This specific story can be found in 2 Samuel 11-12.

04. David, Part One… Humility
General Discussion Questions

Core:

1. How would you characterize your teenage years? How do you think others characterized you when you were a teenager?

2. Why are we so confused and lacking in answers for what it means to 'be a man'?

3. Read 1 Samuel 13:14. What does it mean to be a man *after God's own heart*?

4. What does God look for (and desire to see) in a man's heart?

5. What kind of changes do you need to make in your life in order for God to call you 'a man after his own heart'?

6. Read 1 Samuel 17:33-37. How are David's *identity*, *integrity*, *strength*, and *wisdom* all evidenced here? Do you think it's clear that David is a man after God's own heart?

7. After David sleeps with Bathsheba, do you *still* think it's clear that David is a man after God's own heart?

8. Read 2 Samuel 12:1-13. Do you see Nathan's confrontation with David as loving? If so, why? If not, why?

9. Read 2 Samuel 12:13. What does David's reaction say about his relationship with God?

10. Have you ever been confronted by someone whom you have wronged? Have you ever had to confront someone who has wronged you? How did you react to those confrontations?

11. Does David's example of humility differ from most people's opinion of what it means to be humble?

12. How do you often respond to your own mistakes?

13. What does humility look like during the aftermath of your mistakes?

14. Why do you think God allows us to deal with the consequences of our sins?

15. Read Hebrews 12:5-7. Discuss the similarities and differences between the way God disciplines his children and the way we discipline ours.

16. Read James 4:6. How does God's grace work in your life?

Challenge:

1. Pray about the mistakes you have made, and ask God to help you become truly humble.

2. Demonstrate God's love to others by extending grace when they make mistakes.

04. David, Part One… Humility
Discussion Questions for Women

Core:

1. In 1 Samuel 16:7, God compares the value of appearance to the value of the heart. How does appearance shape a woman's identity?

2. Are women more or less dependent upon appearance for their identity than men?

3. God describes David as 'a man after God's own heart'. If that were all you knew about David, what kind of man would you picture?

4. What do you think God means when he says 'a man after God's own heart'?

5. Read 1 Samuel 13:14. What does it look like to be a woman after God's own heart?

6. How would you compare and contrast David with Samson?

7. Read 2 Samuel 12:1-13. What are some of the consequences of David's sin that he had to live with? What consequences have you been forced to deal with throughout your life?

8. So far, throughout this book, what have you learned about the true definition of womanliness?

9. Think about how God might describe you right now. Is that the way you'd like to be described by God?

Challenge:

- Pray about the changes you can make to become a woman *after God's own heart.*

05.
David, Part Two... Learning From Mistakes

By
Jim Burgen

05.
David, Part Two… Learning From Mistakes

  Even though David made an enormous, life-changing mistake, God never turned his back on him. God didn't change his mind about David, bail on David, or quit loving David. Instead, as a form of loving discipline, God revealed David's sin. David responded to this revelation with humility. He examined his sin and humbly admitted, *This is my fault. I made a terrible decision, and I take full responsibility.*

  Humility is the first half of a pair of characteristics often missing in our lives, and if we want to become men and women after God's own heart, then humility is the perfect place to start.

  But…

  Just because you are humble, admit to your failures, beg for forgiveness, and swear never to repeat your terrible mistakes… and just because God forgives you absolutely… this doesn't mean there won't be any consequences for your sins. In other words, you won't go to hell for your sins, but your life might feel like hell for a while.

  Even if you are genuinely sorry for your mistakes and

humbled by your choices, your humility doesn't amount to anything if you don't continue to pay attention and learn from those mistakes. You must be willing to make adjustments in your life in order to ensure that you won't make the same choices over and over again. After making a poor decision (and you *will* make poor decisions), your first step should be humility: *I admit that I made a mistake… I'm sorry, please forgive me.* But it's essential to follow humility with a willingness to learn from your mistakes: *God, what do you want to teach me? What am I learning through the disaster of my sin's consequences? What do I need to change so that I never walk down this road again?*

    A willingness to learn from mistakes is the second half of humility. You must be humble *and* teachable. If you don't become teachable, then it's only a matter of time until you repeat your mistakes and compound your consequences.

    Be careful not to fall into a life of repetition:

Did you make a mistake?
Yes, I made a mistake… no excuses.
Are you sorry?
Yeah, I'm sorry.
Are you going to do it again?
Yeah, probably.
Why?
Because… that's what I always do. I'm a broken record.

    You aren't doomed to a dull, destructive cycle of mistakes and failures. A better way exists, but will you choose it? When you combine humility with a willingness to learn from your mistakes, you can break the cycle:

Did you make a mistake?
Yes, I made a mistake… no excuses.
Are you sorry?

Yeah, I'm sorry.
Are you going to do it again?
No.
Why?
Because… I'm teachable. I've learned from my bad decisions. I'm paying attention. I want something different. I saw where I went wrong, and I've changed my habits so that I won't repeat my mistakes.

Doesn't that sound like a better way?

A (mostly) teachable man

David – the man after God's own heart – made many mistakes. Sometimes, these mistakes were accidents. More often, these mistakes were intentional. But regardless of his history of sin, David always responded appropriately to his failures. Psalm 51, a song written by David, describes how he responded to his own sin:

> **(1) Have mercy on me, O God,**
>   **according to your unfailing love;**
> **according to your great compassion**
>   **blot out my transgressions.**
> **(2) Wash away all my iniquity**
>   **and cleanse me from my sin.**
> **(3) For I know my transgressions,**
>   **and my sin is always before me.**
> **(Psalm 51:1-3)**

David begged for forgiveness, recognized God's unfailing compassion, and trusted in God's power to forgive. David knew all about his own transgressions, which is a knowledge many of us can identify with. We know what we've done. We don't need to go to church to remind us of our sins. Our failures already haunt our relationships, thoughts, and lives... they touch everything... they are always before us.

> **Against you, you only, have I sinned**
> **and done what is evil in your sight,**
> **so that you are proved right when you speak**
> **and justified when you judge. (Psalm 51:4)**

We can ruin the lives of our families, we can lose our jobs, and we can destroy our friendships, but ultimately, we sin against God. When we sin, we offend God – the only being who is justified in his judgment. When we mess up, God has the absolute right to speak up and give us what we deserve. Thankfully, our God is a merciful God, but we couldn't blame him for dishing out the punishment we deserve.

> **Surely I was sinful at birth,**
> **sinful from the time my mother conceived me.**
> **(Psalm 51:5)**

Timeout. Don't panic, and don't let this verse freak you out. This verse doesn't claim that, when a baby dies, that baby goes to hell because of his or her inherent sin. Many people have twisted this verse to support that concept, but that concept is a lie. Instead, David is saying, *Sometimes, it feels that I am wired – right down to my core DNA – to screw up. Sometimes, it feels like I'm not even trying to sin... but I rebel against the truth anyway.*

We can all identify with this overwhelming feeling of inevitable failure, can't we? Most of the time, we aren't trying to screw up. Do you ever wake up in the morning and say, *Man... I hope I sin more than I did yesterday*? Do you ever go to bed at night thinking, *Man... I tried to sin today, but I couldn't come up with one*?

Of course not! No parent needed to teach his or her kid to break the rules. From the moment that crying, squirming baby came home from the hospital, it was over. The minute they could speak, they were yelling, *No!!!* You didn't have to teach your kids to keep hitting their brothers and sisters – they were ready to fight from the time they could make fists. We began breaking rules the moment we took our first breaths, and this is the truth to which David refers.

> **(6) Surely you desire truth in the inner parts;**
> **you teach me wisdom in the inmost place.**
> **(13) Then I will teach transgressors your ways,**
> **and sinners will turn back to you.**
> **(Psalm 51:6, 13)**

David realized he was teachable. He told God that he was listening and ready to receive wisdom. Then, he promised to take the lessons he would learn and reveal them to the people he loved. David not only promised to learn from his mistakes, but also to teach others not to repeat the same, bad decisions.

Doesn't that sound like a better way? Obviously, life would be better if we never made another mistake, but realistically, that will never happen. Therefore, we need to learn how to cope with our mistake-filled lives. When we make mistakes, will we react with humility or defensiveness? When we make mistakes, will we repeat ourselves or become teachable? Will we be able to learn from the messes we crawl through?

Most of the time, David was humble *and* teachable – he was even willing to teach others the lessons he learned from his own mistakes – but there was one area of David's life that took him a *long* time to learn from. I want to discuss this part of David's life for two reasons. First, I want to further illustrate how much is at stake in our lives when we sin. The consequences of sin can be utterly devastating. You might have pushed the lead domino over, but you don't get to control how far the destruction stretches. Second, I want to show what can happen if we don't become teachable. No matter how awful you think your life has become, if you refuse to learn from your mistakes, or if you misapply the lessons you've learned from your mistakes, then your life can get much, *much* more painful.

A story of inaction

Life would be hard enough if, when we made mistakes, the weight of the consequences fell solely on our own heads. Sadly, this isn't the case. Instead, when we make mistakes, the weight of the consequences falls not only on our own heads, but also on the heads of everyone around us… everyone we care about… everyone we love. Sometimes, the consequences land even harder on those that we love.

David learned this lesson the hard way. Nathan warned David that the consequences of his sin would fall heavily on David's kingdom, home, marriage, and (especially) children. Nathan also made very clear that these consequences were not a product of God's anger, wrath, or lust for punishment, but were simply a natural result of David's mistakes. If fact, Nathan told David he was forgiven. But being forgiven for your sin doesn't mean that you get to control the consequences of that sin. The natural result of sin is the devastation of relationships and the ruin of lives. That might sound harsh, mean, or unfair, but I'm sorry… it's just the truth.

Thankfully, God promises that if we stay humble, pay attention, and become teachable, then he will help us survive the destruction caused by our sin.

Let's pick David's story back up:

In the course of time, Amnon son of David fell in love with Tamar, the beautiful sister of Absalom son of David. (2 Samuel 13:1)

This verse requires some explanation. This story took place several years after the whole Bathsheba-Uriah-adultery-murder thing. By this time, David had multiple wives – maybe six or seven. Polygamy has never been a part of God's plan for anybody, but at this point in history, when two kings made a deal, that deal might sound something like this, *I'll give you some soldiers if you give me your daughter and two hundred acres of land.* This system of barter was immoral and against scriptural teaching, but the kings practiced it anyway.

David was married to six or seven different women, and he had different children with each of these wives. Therefore, David had a son (Amnon) with one wife, and he had a son and a daughter (Absalom and Tamar, respectively) with another wife. To connect these confusing dots, Amnon is Tamar's half-brother.

Amnon became frustrated to the point of illness on account of his sister Tamar, for she was a virgin, and it seemed impossible for him to do anything to her. (2 Samuel 13:2)

Wherever you think this story is headed… you are *exactly* right. Incest was as gross back then as it is now, but regardless, Amnon wanted to have sex with his half-sister, Tamar.

(3) Now Amnon had a friend named Jonadab son of Shimeah, David's brother. Jonadab was a very shrewd man. (4) He asked Amnon, "Why do you, the king's son, look so

haggard morning after morning? Won't you tell me?"
 Amnon said to him, "I'm in love with Tamar, my brother Absalom's sister." (2 Samuel 13:3-4)

 Let's try to keep these family relations straight: Jonadab was Amnon's cousin. Jonadab was also a shrewd man. When an author of the Bible uses the word 'shrewd' to describe a person, that author is trying to convey a slimy, sneaky jerk. In other words, Jonadab was a creep. Also, keep in mind that Amnon was not truly in love with Tamar. He was only turned on. He only wanted sex.

 (5) "Go to bed and pretend to be ill," Jonadab said. "When your father comes to see you, say to him, 'I would like my sister Tamar to come and give me something to eat. Let her prepare the food in my sight so I may watch her and then eat it from her hand.'"
 (6) So Amnon lay down and pretended to be ill. When the king came to see him, Amnon said to him, "I would like my sister Tamar to come and make some special bread in my sight, so I may eat from her hand."
 (7) David sent word to Tamar at the palace: "Go to the house of your brother Amnon and prepare some food for him." **(8)** So Tamar went to the house of her brother Amnon, who was lying down. She took some dough, kneaded it, made the bread in his sight and baked it. **(9)** Then she took the pan and served him the bread, but he refused to eat.
 "Send everyone out of here," Amnon said. So everyone left him. **(10)** Then Amnon said to Tamar, "Bring the food here into my bedroom so I may eat from your hand." And Tamar took the bread she had prepared and brought it to her brother Amnon in his bedroom. **(11)** But when she took it to him to eat, he grabbed her and said, "Come to bed with me, my sister."
 (12) "Don't, my brother!" she said to him. "Don't

force me. Such a thing should not be done in Israel! Don't do this wicked thing. (13) What about me? Where could I get rid of my disgrace? And what about you? You would be like one of the wicked fools in Israel. Please speak to the king; he will not keep me from being married to you." (14) But he refused to listen to her, and since he was stronger than she, he raped her.

(15) Then Amnon hated her with intense hatred. In fact, he hated her more than he had loved her. Amnon said to her, "Get up and get out!"

(16) "No!" she said to him. "Sending me away would be a greater wrong than what you have already done to me."

But he refused to listen to her. (17) He called his personal servant and said, "Get this woman out of here and bolt the door after her." (18) So his servant put her out and bolted the door after her. She was wearing a richly ornamented robe, for this was the kind of garment the virgin daughters of the king wore. (19) Tamar put ashes on her head and tore the ornamented robe she was wearing. She put her hand on her head and went away, weeping aloud as she went.

(20) Her brother Absalom said to her, "Has that Amnon, your brother, been with you? Be quiet now, my sister; he is your brother. Don't take this thing to heart." And Tamar lived in her brother Absalom's house, a desolate woman.

(21) When King David heard all this, he was furious. (22) Absalom never said a word to Amnon, either good or bad; he hated Amnon because he had disgraced his sister Tamar. (2 Samuel 13:5-22)

Did you catch David's reaction to this whole mess? *When King David heard all this, he was furious.* Seriously? One of David's sons raped his own sister, and David's only response was anger? *If you rape my daughter, I'll get cranky!* Really? That's it?

As the father of a daughter, I'm dumbfounded by David's response. Why would a man, a father – a king! – totally drop the ball on something this big? I'm not suggesting David should have had Amnon killed (even though he murdered Uriah for less), but come on! Somebody needed his tail kicked! If someone ever raped *my* daughter – and I can't let my head go too far down this road – I don't know what I'd do! But I definitely know that someone would get their rear-end handed to them (I cleaned that up for this book… I'm trying to be more teachable). First, it's simply a horrible thing to do to someone. The monstrosity of the act alone is reason enough to seek action. Second, my daughter needs to know that I'll be there for her. I'll stand up for her and protect her.

David did *nothing*. He didn't even ground Amnon or have a talk with him. He simply got angry. Why was David so locked up?

There are only two possible explanations I can come up with for David's inaction: *bad guilt* and *bad grace*.

Bad guilt

Have you ever known the type of person who, upon witnessing the mistreatment of someone they love, only responds with, *Well… who am I to say anything? I made the same mistakes myself when I was their age. I don't have any right to give a lecture.*

Are you this type of person? Maybe bad guilt was running through David's mind: *I messed up sexually when I was* younger, so I'm not really qualified to hand out advice to my son. He's going to have to learn the hard way just like I did.

There's another destructive aspect to bad guilt. I'm pretty sure that if David really *had* reproached Amnon, then Amnon would have responded with the following: *Are you talking to me, you hypocrite? Can I remind you of the whole Bathsheba disaster that wrecked our entire family? Who are you to lecture me?*

In other words: *What is your identity, David? And how are you going to live up to that identity? Who are you, David?*

By the way, here is the biblically appropriate answer to that question: *Amnon, I'm your father. You're right... I screwed up a huge part of my life, but God taught me a lot through that experience, and I'm not going to idly stand by and do nothing as you make the same mistakes I made. You're right... I messed up... no excuses... and now I'm living with the consequences. But as your father, I'm not allowed to say, "Sorry, I'm disqualified." I'm supposed to take what I've experienced and lovingly speak into your life. So... sit your butt down because we need to work through this mess.*

Can you tell this is a bit of a soapbox for me? I spent twenty years in youth ministry, and I've heard some pretty idiotic comments come from some of the kids' parents. Comments like, *I'm not really qualified to give my kid advice,* and, *I made the same mistakes when I was a kid, so I have no room to speak up.* Here's one of my favorites: *I don't want to shove Jesus down his throat... I don't want to make her go to church like my parents did to me.*

If making mistakes truly disqualified us from leading our children, then we should all put our kids up for adoption. We should all resign from parenthood. Everybody makes mistakes. We aren't talking about whether or not you've made mistakes. We are talking about how you respond to those mistakes. Your response can change your kid's life.

If your parents tried to shove Jesus down your throat, and he didn't taste good, that's because they were trying to feed you a bad Jesus. The *real* Jesus is awesome. If your last church was a dud, and you never wanted to go, then I'm sorry. But I can vouch for Flatirons – it's not a bad place – so shut up, get your kids in the car, and head to church. You know what that's called? It's called *good parenting*.

Here's the point: bad guilt is robbing you. Bad guilt is keeping you from being a leader to the most important people in your life. Guilt can be good. Guilt can be a gift. Guilt is like a hot flame – it's *supposed* to hurt. But guilt only causes pain so that it gets your attention. After its got your attention, you are supposed pull your hand away from that flame. You are supposed to pull yourself away from the things that are burning your life. Guilt was never meant to be something that you carry around indefinitely. If you carry that kind of guilt for too long, then you will eventually burn down your home.

Guilt was never meant to ruin or run your life. You screwed up… trust me, I know what that's like. But God has forgiven us, and now we need to forgive ourselves. We need to re-enter the lives of the people who need us the most. We need to resume a roll of leadership for our families' sakes.

Bad grace

Bad grace is another reason I believe David failed as a leader, a man, and a father. Don't get me wrong – I *love* grace. But there is a bad version of grace floating around. Some Christians have taken the concept of God's forgiveness and twisted it so they believe they have no right to speak truth into other people's lives. Some people have misapplied grace: *I made some terrible mistakes, but God forgave me. I don't have any right to try to help you fix your life. After all, God did everything for me, and he'll do everything for you. So keep on doing whatever you want, and eventually, God will forgive you.*

Some of us have the 'it's all good' approach to God's grace: *Do whatever you want because, in the end, it will all work out. God will forgive you of anything, so it doesn't matter how you act right now.*

To be honest, sometimes I wish that were true… but it's not. Nowhere in the Bible do you find a single instance of God saying to someone, *Okay, I forgive you, so go ahead and continue repeating the same mistakes over and over because I have so much grace! Your actions don't matter because I'll keep on forgiving you! Have fun!*

The Bible actually says the opposite. After describing who Jesus is and what he can do for his believers, Paul (a guy who, at one point, royally messed up his own life) says:

(1) What shall we say, then? Shall we go on sinning so that grace may increase? (2) By no means! We died to sin; how can we live in it any longer? (Romans 6:1-2)

Paul asks the following question: *Since we have unlimited grace and forgiveness from God, should we continue sinning? Should we keep repeating the same mistakes? God has promised to forgive us for anything. Does this mean we have free reign to do whatever we want?*

Then, Paul answers his own question: *By no means! No way! Grace is available to those who have died to sin. Grace is available to those who want, more than anything, to stop the vicious cycle of sin in their lives. Grace isn't available to those who want to continue living in their own filth.*

In other words, if your approach to life is, *Jesus will always bail me out of my mess, so I don't care how I live my life, and I don't need to change anything about my habits*, then you've completely missed who Jesus is and what he is teaching.

Missing the point is bad enough, but it gets worse. When you misapply God's grace, the people in your life who desperately need you to speak truth will begin to follow your example. They will begin to expect God's grace as a reward for not taking responsibility for their own actions, and they will begin walking down the dangerous path of cheap, bad grace.

There are so many people who are trapped in bad marriages because the abusive or cheating spouse continually throws the 'grace card' on the table: *You can't expect me to change. You have to put up with me and continually forgive me because, if you don't, you'll become a hypocrite.*

For some of us, this is our story. I've lost count of the number of women who approach me in the lobby after a weekend service and tell me that people have used Jesus *against* them… they've only known Jesus as an 'ace in the hole' that their spouses play in order to win arguments.

How many more of our friends, parents, or children are going to continue blowing up their lives while we, like David, stand by and watch?[1]

How long?

David's story actually gets worse. *How could it get worse? His son raped his daughter!* Trust me, it gets worse.

Two years after the rape, Absalom made good on his personal promise to kill Amnon. After Absalom murdered his brother, David repeated his lack of initiative – he did nothing! Absalom then lost all respect for David and began to view his father as a weak man. Eventually, Absalom took all of David's wives onto the roof of the palace and had sex with them in front of all of Israel. Then, after he finished, he stood up and mocked his dad. *See! My dad won't do anything. He ought to do what's right, but he won't because he's weak. He's a wimp. In fact, I would be a better king than David.*

Absalom then attempted to conquer the throne, but wound up with three javelins through his heart.

I sometimes wonder how different David's story would have been had he only taken action with his sons. Eventually, David got rid of his bad guilt and bad grace, but two sons had to die and a daughter's life had to be ruined before David became teachable. David's family had been torn to shreds before he finally had an '*aha!*' moment, woke up, and realized, *Maybe I'm not doing the dad thing very well… maybe something needs to change.*

I want to end these two chapters about David with a series of questions:

How long before we finally learn from David's story? How much more do we have to lose? How bad does it have to get before we finally examine our lives and say, *Enough! I get it! I will learn to be teachable. I need to change my habits. I won't lead my family down this path anymore*?

How long?

How long before we break the cords of bad guilt that have bound our hands? How long before we realize that grace is not a 'get out of jail free' card that can be used at our own discretion? How long before we quit using bad guilt and bad grace as excuses to sit idly by and refuse the responsibility of leadership?

Our marriages, kids, and friendships are at stake. Our happiness is at stake. Our lives are at stake.

What areas of your life need to change in order to ensure your family's safety and happiness? We all have aspects of our lives that need work, so what is yours? I know that the defenses are beginning to reveal themselves: *Jim, are you saying that if I don't step up to the plate and do the right thing, then I'm not a real man?*

Yes. In fact, I'm not saying that… God is. *I'm* tempted to call you a middle-aged, little boy. The people who truly need you – your wife, kids, friends, or girlfriend – have enough little boys in their lives. What they need is a man. More than that… what they need is a man after God's own heart.

How long will it take to change?

I know this is heavy and intimidating, so let me throw an umbrella over this whole teaching: *Me too.*

Me too. I'm not there yet either. I'm not throwing any stones. In fact, I can safely say that it's never too late because I can genuinely relate to the overwhelming pressure of biblical manhood. It's never too late to begin becoming a man after God's own heart. We can't change our pasts. We can't control the consequences of our sins.

But…

With God's grace, mercy, love, and strength, we *can*

alter our futures. We can become teachable men and women of God, we can learn from our mistakes, and we can ensure that our futures won't become mirror images of our pasts. When we combine humility with the willingness to learn from our mistakes, God will begin to heal our lives.

1. See **Appendix: A note on parental discipline** for further discussion on God's loving discipline.

05. David, Part Two… Learning From Mistakes
General Discussion Questions

Core:

    1. Discuss the highlights and lowlights of David's life. How did the presence or absence of certain character qualities dictate his circumstances?

    2. Do you believe that God never changes his mind about loving you? Do you believe that there is nothing we can do that will shock God? If those statements were true, what difference would they make in your life?

    3. A person's life is not destroyed as much by the mistakes they make, but more by the decisions they make after their mistakes. Have you seen this truth play out in your own life or the lives of others?

    4. Read Psalm 51. What was David's perspective on God and God's forgiveness?

    5. Even though he was forgiven, David experienced the consequences of his sins and mistakes for the rest of his life. Is this fair?

    6. In your own words, describe your understanding of bad guilt and bad grace.

    7. Read Romans 6:1-2, and discuss the questions that Paul raises.

    8. Read Proverbs 13:24, and discuss the loving nature of God's discipline.

9. How can you cultivate humility and a willingness to learn from your mistakes?

Challenge:

1. Think about someone who needs you to be more of a man in his or her life, and begin taking steps in that direction.

2. Pay attention and meditate on what God is teaching you through his Word and through your circumstances.

05. David, Part Two... Learning From Mistakes Discussion Questions for Women

Core:

1. Have you ever been in a situation where you've suffered the consequences of someone else's mistakes? Have the consequences of your own mistakes ever fallen on the heads of those closest to you?

2. What does it mean to be teachable in your spiritual life?

3. As a woman, what is your initial response to the story of David's daughter and two sons in 2 Samuel 13:1-21?

4. When does guilt serve a positive purpose? When does guilt become *bad guilt*?

5. In your experience, are women more prone to *bad guilt* than men? Why or why not?

6. David was a weak parent. What has your experience looked like in terms of parents speaking into your life? Have you had weak parents or strong parents? In what ways have your parents shaped you?

7. Are there people waiting for you to step up as a mom, daughter, sister, or friend, and speak truth into their lives?

8. As a grown woman, who or what has shaped you the most since you were a child?

9. If more men were to live up to God's intentions for their lives, how would this change the lives of women? If more

women were to live up to God's intentions for their lives, how would this change the lives of men?

Challenge:

1. Spend some time taking inventory of people in your life who need you to step up and speak truth to them.

2. Spend some time studying Psalm 51. Pray that God will make you teachable and use you to teach others.

06.
Boaz… Honor and Protectiveness

By
Scott Nickell

06.
Boaz... Honor and Protectiveness

While we could probably write on the subject of biblical manhood for decades, we figured that no one would want to pick up a sixty-pound book called *Grow A Pair*, so it's time to wrap this up.

To do so, I want to examine the life of a lesser-known man in the Bible: Boaz. Until this chapter, we have talked about some fairly prominent characters of the Bible – Joseph, Samson, and David. Those are names and stories that, even if you've never spent a day in church, you've probably heard before. Boaz is different. In fact, I wouldn't be surprised if some people who *have* spent a lot of time in church are still not familiar with the story of Boaz.

Regardless of his popularity, Boaz was a *real* man, and he exemplified the last pair of characteristics we're going to discuss in this book: *honor* and *protectiveness*.

Ruth and Naomi

Before diving into this story, I need to offer some context. The story of Boaz can be found in a little book of the

Bible named Ruth. Ruth and Boaz's story takes place during the same time frame as Samson's story in the Book of Judges. Therefore, as you remember from the chapter on Samson, this was a time when God's people were, on a national level, continually treading through a cycle of pain, tragedy, hope, and deliverance. The story of Boaz and Ruth reflects this same cycle, but on a more personal, intimate level.

Let's jump in:

(1) In the days when the judges ruled, there was a famine in the land, and a man from Bethlehem in Judah, together with his wife and two sons, went to live for a while in the country of Moab. (2) The man's name was Elimelech, his wife's name Naomi, and the names of his two sons were Mahlon and Kilion. They were Ephrathites from Bethlehem, Judah. And they went to Moab and lived there.
(3) Now Elimelech, Naomi's husband, died, and she was left with her two sons. (4) They married Moabite women, one named Orpah and the other Ruth. After they had lived there about ten years, (5) both Mahlon and Kilion also died, and Naomi was left without her two sons and her husband. (Ruth 1:1-5)

A man named Elimelech lived in a town called Bethlehem – a town that may sound vaguely familiar to some of us. Due to a great famine, Elimelech moved himself, his wife, and his two sons to a neighboring town called Moab. From the outside, his decision appeared to be a sound one. Moab received much more annual rainfall, and it had a number of natural springs, streams, and rivers. Moab would be a logical place to move if your hometown was being ruined by drought and famine.

However, there was a dark side to Elimelech's decision, as well. Not only did the people of Bethlehem have a history of conflict with the people of Moab, but the Moabites also worshipped a false god named Chemosh. Moving to Moab should have been a big '*no-no*' to a guy like Elimelech, but he panicked and took the risk anyway.

The tragedy of this story compounds quickly. Shortly after the move to Moab, Elimelech died and left his wife, Naomi, in one of the most vulnerable positions a woman of this culture could find herself: a foreign widow. Naomi found comfort under the protection of her two sons, but they, too, died ten years later. Naomi was left in a foreign land, away from any family connection, with no husband or sons, and with two daughters-in-law to take care of. To make the situation worse, Naomi's daughters-in-law had been childless for ten years. For a culture with no means of birth control, this probably meant that both women were barren. Barrenness is not only devastating for any woman, but in Ruth and Naomi's male-dominant culture, being barren also meant that there was no hope of a future son who could re-establish their social positions – their family name and lineage ended with them.

Let's fast-forward the story a bit. People began to view Naomi as a cursed woman… someone whom the planets had aligned against… someone with whom God *must* be angry. Naomi allowed those voices to define her identity, and she began to view herself in the same way. Eventually, Naomi believed that her only option was to return, with her daughters-in-law, to her homeland in hopes that someone would be kind to her. So Naomi and her two daughters-in-law, Orpah and Ruth, gathered their few possessions and began the journey to Bethlehem.

Not long into the journey, Naomi came to the startling realization that, by taking Orpah and Ruth to Bethlehem, her daughters-in-law would become widows in a foreign land – the very same social position that Naomi herself was running from.

Naomi stopped mid-journey and said to Orpah and Ruth, *I love you very much, but I think it would be better for you to turn back and restart your lives in Moab. Go find husbands, and settle down in your homeland.* The two daughters-in-law began crying and asking to stay, but Naomi was resolute. Eventually, Orpah turned back and headed for home, but Ruth clung to Naomi and said, *No way. I will go wherever you go. I will worship whomever you worship. Until I die, I'm sticking with you.* Naomi quickly understood that there would be no changing Ruth's mind, so the two women continued their journey to Bethlehem.

When Ruth and Naomi finally arrived at Bethlehem, there was a great stir. The town, at the time, was small – maybe just a couple hundred people – and they all knew and remembered Naomi. They most likely viewed Naomi as a traitor who bailed on Bethlehem when times got tough. They were probably saying, *Look at you now. You got what you deserved. You've come back from Moab with no husband, no son, and only a strange, foreign girl? You had this coming.*

This was a bitter moment for Naomi. Look at her response:

(20) "Don't call me Naomi," she told them. "Call me Mara, because the Almighty has made my life very bitter. (21) I went away full, but the Lord has brought me back empty. Why call me Naomi? The Lord has afflicted me; the Almighty has brought misfortune upon me." (Ruth 1:20-21)

The name 'Naomi' means, "pleasant," and the name 'Mara' means, "bitter." Obviously, Naomi was in a place of incredible anger toward God. She found herself in an emotional state that many of us can easily identify with. She was angry with God, so she decided to point the finger at him: *You forgot about me. You turned your back on me. I feel empty, and I have no hope… thanks a lot.*

I've done this before. Who hasn't? Oftentimes, we blame God for the circumstances that were birthed by our own poor decisions because it's easier than pointing the finger at ourselves. However, at that point in Naomi's life, she couldn't see that God had a specific plan developed for her future – a plan that she could never have predicted.

Boaz – A man of honor

This is where our story gets interesting, and this is where we meet the man I want to discuss: Boaz.

Now Naomi had a relative on her husband's side, from the clan of Elimelech, a man of standing, whose name was Boaz. (Ruth 2:1)

Right away, we learn two important things about Boaz. First of all, he was a relative of Elimelech, Naomi's husband. As we'll discover in a moment, this is crucial information. Second, the Bible describes Boaz as, "a man of standing." This Hebrew phrase can be translated many different ways in the Old Testament – here are a few: "worthy man; man of valor; man of wealth; mighty man; or, very able." This phrase broadly communicates at least four important aspects of Boaz's character: he was a man of strength, courage, ability, and success. To simplify, Boaz was a man of *honor*. Boaz had a solid reputation. He was the type of man that other men looked up to. He was honorable.

Before continuing Boaz and Ruth's story, let me pose a question: *How does a person become honorable?* Or, maybe this is a better phrasing: *Can you decide, as you are holding this book, to suddenly become honorable?*

No. Sorry, but no. You don't become honorable – or dishonorable – overnight. No husband or wife wakes up one morning and suddenly decides, out of the blue, to cheat on his or her spouse. No mother or father wakes up one morning and suddenly decides, out of the blue, to abuse his or her children. Instead, a strand of smaller, poor decisions culminates in those larger, life-altering decisions.

Trust me, I'm not throwing stones. *Me too.* There are character flaws that I'm still trying to pry out of my life. I wish I could tell you that I'm totally different from the selfish, childish, temperamental, little boy that my wife married when I was twenty years old, but I'm not. Sure, I'm different. But I'm not *totally* different. I can still be childish sometimes. I'll be the first to confess that I'm the most selfish person I know. I wish I could say that, every night I come home from work, I spend hours of quality time with my family. I wish I could say I spend every night cherishing and appreciating my kids as blessings from God, but truthfully, there are many nights when I put them to bed as soon as possible in order to sit in my recliner, watch television, and talk to no one. After ten hard years of earnestly trying to become more honorable, I can still lose my temper, I can still be a control freak, and I can still be lazy in my marriage. Moving toward honor is a long, slow process, and we have to partner with God as he changes us from the inside out.

Which direction are you heading? Are you taking steps toward a life of honor, or are you taking steps toward a life of dishonor? A man doesn't, overnight, turn from being an honorable husband, dad, friend, son, or brother to being a dishonorable one. Instead, dishonor is created by a laundry list of small compromises that gradually grow bigger and bigger. In other words, the diminishing return of sin always leads to the escalation of risk.

The diminishing return of sin always leads to the escalation of risk.

For example, the diminishing return of financial sin always leads to the escalation of risk. Over the years, we've witnessed many CEOs end up in prison. That didn't happen overnight. I doubt that any CEO began their career saying, *I hope I end up cheating people at every turn, exploiting my employees, and sneaking away with as much illegal profit as I possibly can!* No… instead, they began with ignoring a few, little discrepancies in financial statements and tax returns. When that was no longer rewarding enough, the risk continually escalated until they found themselves involved in elaborate schemes and cover-ups.

Another example: the diminishing return of sexual sin always leads to the escalation of risk. I don't think anyone has ever been married with the intention of blowing up his or her relationship as soon as possible: *I think I'll lie, steal, and cheat until this whole marriage things goes up in smoke!* No… instead, most affairs today begin in front of a computer. A few minutes of surfing Internet porn quickly lead to a few hours. A few days out of the week spent surfing Internet porn quickly lead to everyday of the week. Each time becomes less rewarding as the returns gradually diminish, so the risk bumps up: *What if I start chatting with her online? What if, while I'm out of town, I go to a strip club? What if, while I'm in this hotel room, I skim the telephone book for 'escort services'?*

The risk continues to escalate because sin, by definition, only offers continually diminishing returns, and suddenly, what was once unimaginable is now a genuine consideration. I guarantee that no man or woman has ever *accidentally* ended up in the arms of the wrong person. There is always a long string of poor decisions and compromises that led that individual perfectly into his or her arms.

You don't become dishonorable overnight. Likewise, you don't become honorable overnight. Honor begins with being honest on your taxes when you're barely making $20,000 a year. Honor begins with being honest on your taxes when you're easily making more than $200,000 a year. Honor begins with flipping the channel, turning off the computer, and going to bed with your wife, if you have one – alone, if you don't.

You don't become honorable or dishonorable overnight, and there is hope in this truth. Some of us may be thinking, *Scott, my reputation precedes me. I've blown up just about everything and everyone in my life. 'Honorable' is not the adjective anyone would ever use to describe me. Getting to a place of honor is a mountain far too big for me to climb.* That might seem like the truth, but you need to remember that you can't climb that mountain overnight; it's impossible. Every great journey starts with a single step. Small decisions headed in the right direction can lead to a big change. Small decisions headed in the right direction can lead to a life of honor.

Boaz – A protective man

Enough about us… let's get back to Boaz. The Bible describes Boaz as, "a man of standing." In other words, over the course of his life, Boaz had exhibited the godly characteristics we've covered throughout this book: identity, integrity, strength, wisdom, humility, and a willingness to learn from his mistakes. Let's continue his story:

(2) And Ruth the Moabitess said to Naomi, "Let me go to the fields and pick up the leftover grain behind anyone in whose eyes I find favor."
Naomi said to her, "Go ahead, my daughter." (3) So she went out and began to glean in the fields behind the

harvesters. As it turned out, she found herself working in a field belonging to Boaz, who was from the clan of Elimelech. (Ruth 2:2-3)

Ruth and Naomi arrived in Bethlehem during the time of harvest. In Hebrew culture, when a man harvested his field, he never went back over that field a second time. Whatever fell on the ground, he would leave for the poor to come and glean. Furthermore, he didn't harvest to the very edges of his field. Basically, he didn't squeeze every last drop from his land. Instead, he left those crops for the most marginalized, unfortunate, and vulnerable members of society; in this case, widows, orphans, and foreigners. These were laws given by God through Moses, and they provide a beautiful picture of a society working together to take care of its poor and vulnerable.

At this point in the story, Ruth was gleaning the fields for leftover food to take home for Naomi and herself.

(4) Just then Boaz arrived from Bethlehem and greeted the harvesters, "The Lord be with you!"
"The Lord bless you!" they called back.
(5) Boaz asked the foreman of his harvesters, "Whose young woman is that?"
(6) The foreman replied, "She is the Moabitess who came back from Moab with Naomi. (7) She said, 'Please let me glean and gather among the sheaves behind the harvesters.' She went into the field and has worked steadily from morning till now, except for a short rest in the shelter."
(8) So Boaz said to Ruth, "My daughter, listen to me. Don't go and glean in another field and don't go away from here. Stay here with my servant girls. (9) Watch the field where the men are harvesting, and follow along after the girls. I have told the men not to touch you. And whenever you are thirsty, go and get a drink from the water jars the men have filled." (Ruth 2:4-9)

We notice another admirable characteristic of Boaz in these verses. Boaz was *protective*. Similar to our own culture, it was not uncommon in Boaz's culture for the poor to be taken advantage of. In Boaz's society, Ruth was a beautiful, young, foreign widow, and she would have been vulnerable to rape. However, Boaz valued her greatly and leveraged his strength, power, influence, and honorable reputation in order to protect Ruth. Can you picture this scenario? Boaz gathered all of his male workers together and said, *Hey, gentlemen… huddle up. Did you notice that new, pretty Moabite girl over there? Yeah… don't touch her. Lay a finger on her, and you'll answer to me.*

Why does this picture of Boaz's protectiveness cause some of our hearts to well up? Why do we want to applaud Boaz? There are several reasons this image of protectiveness provokes such a tender response. First, there are some men who are thinking, *Right on! That's the way it's done!* Men have a deep, natural sense of divine responsibility to protect women. Protectiveness is a God-given inclination for men.

Second, there are some of us who weren't protected like we should have been. We had non-existent, weak, aloof, absentee fathers, and that relationship has left a scar. For some of us, the reason we are so proud of Boaz is the same reason we are so disappointed in David for his weak response to his daughter's rape. Our hearts well up because we long for protective men in our lives. Some of us didn't just have absentee fathers, but we had abusive fathers; there is no sicker perversion of manhood. There is nothing more dishonorable.

Boaz, however, was protective, and his treatment of Ruth was honorable. So here is my question: *What does this type of honor and protectiveness look like today?*

We could go on all day. This type of honor and protectiveness looks like the college guy who, when out with his friends, stops his buddies from taking advantage of the girl who drank too much. That's called growing a pair: *honor* and *protectiveness*.

This type of honor and protectiveness looks like the son who steps between his elderly mom and her manipulative landlord.

This type of honor and protectiveness looks like the dad who says to his daughter and her boyfriend, *No… you're not going to 'watch a movie' in the basement, but you're welcome to watch one in the family room (and I hope my gun collection won't distract you).*

As the father of two boys and one girl, I sense a different level of protectiveness with my daughter. There's no better way to explain it. The same goes for my wife. I never want a single doubt in my family's minds that I will fight for them and protect them in every sense. A real man not only has a deep sense of protectiveness for women, but (like Boaz) he also acts on that natural instinct.

Boaz – A kinsman-redeemer

Boaz acted on his natural inclination toward protectiveness, and Ruth was floored:

(10) At this, she bowed down with her face to the ground. She exclaimed, "Why have I found such favor in your eyes that you notice me – a foreigner?"
(11) Boaz replied, "I've been told all about what you have done for your mother-in-law since the death of your husband – how you left your father and mother and your homeland and came to live with a people you did not know before. **(12)** May the Lord repay you for what you have done. May you be richly rewarded by the Lord, the God of

Israel, under whose wings you have come to take refuge. (Ruth 2:10-12)

That last part is key: *Under whose wings you have come to take refuge.* The image of protective wings is used repeatedly throughout Scripture:

**How priceless is your unfailing love!
Both high and low among men
    find refuge in the shadow of your wings.
(Psalm 36:7)**

**Have mercy on me, O God, have mercy on me,
    for in you my soul takes refuge.
I will take refuge in the shadow of your wings
    until the disaster has passed.
(Psalm 57:1)**

The image in these verses is that of a powerful eagle gathering a young eaglet that can't fly under the protection of its wings. In the Bible, God is often described as one who gathers his people under the wings of his protection. One day, Jesus was looking out across Jerusalem and wept, saying, *I long to gather you under the protection of my wings, but you continue to rebel, and run away from me.*[1]

In a single sentence, Boaz both proclaimed the name of the God he worshiped, the God of Israel, and also explained to Ruth that he was acting on his instinctive sense of protection because he worshiped a God of protection.

Once again, let's fast-forward our story a bit. After Ruth finished working the field, Boaz invited her to eat at his table. They enjoyed dinner together, and Boaz sent Ruth home with leftovers for Naomi. Ruth told Naomi about her experience in Boaz's fields, and Naomi was pleased:

"The Lord bless him!" Naomi said to her daughter-in-law. "He has not stopped showing his kindness to the living and the dead." She added, "That man is our close relative; he is one of our kinsman-redeemers." (Ruth 2:20)

The *kinsman-redeemer* was an interesting concept in Israel. If a man died without any sons to perpetuate the family name, then the closest male relative had a responsibility to marry the man's widow and have sons on his behalf. The kinsman-redeemer was also responsible for buying back any land the family lost.

Naomi realized that Boaz was a close relative, and she believed he could potentially be a kinsman-redeemer for her family. As Ruth spent more time gleaning in Boaz's field, Naomi began to hatch a plan. Finally, she revealed her risky (and quite strange) plan to Ruth:

(1) One day Naomi her mother-in-law said to her, "My daughter, should I not try to find a home for you, where you will be well provided for? (2) Is not Boaz, with whose servant girls you have been, a kinsman of ours? Tonight he will be winnowing barley on the threshing floor. (3) Wash and perfume yourself, and put on your best clothes. Then go down to the threshing floor, but don't let him know you are there until he has finished eating and drinking. (4) When he lies down, note the place where he is lying. Then go and uncover his feet and lie down. He will tell you what to do. (Ruth 3:1-4)

Like I said… this plan was weird. If you grew up going to Sunday school, I can assure you that your teachers never taught this part of the story. Let me sum up what's going on. When the harvest was finishing up, the men would often work late into the night on the threshing floor. When they finally finished, they would throw a huge party to celebrate the end of harvest. Therefore, the threshing floor became a hot spot for prostitutes because it's good for business when men are partying and drinking. So... Naomi said to Ruth, *Take a bath, put on some perfume, head down to the threshing floor, and hang out with Boaz. When he's tired of drinking and decides to lie down, try lying down with him... let's see what he does.*

My first reaction to Naomi's plan is always shock: *Are you kidding me? Really? This is your plan? Lie down next to a buzzed – maybe even drunk – guy, and do whatever he commands? Where is the wisdom in this plan?*

However, I can't help but think that Naomi and Ruth were fairly certain of Boaz's honor. I wonder if they were using this moment – a moment when Boaz would be at his weakest – to test his true honor.

(5) "I will do whatever you say," Ruth answered. (6) So she went down to the threshing floor and did everything her mother-in-law told her to do. (7) When Boaz had finished eating and drinking and was in good spirits, he went over to lie down at the far end of the grain pile. Ruth approached quietly, uncovered his feet and lay down. (8) In the middle of the night something startled the man, and he turned and discovered a woman lying at his feet.
(9) "Who are you?" he asked.
"I am your servant Ruth," she said. "Spread the corner of your garment over me, since you are a kinsman-redeemer." (Ruth 3:5-9)

When Ruth said, "Spread the corner of your garment over me," she used a word for 'corner' that also means 'wings'. Her request can literally be translated, "Spread your wings over your servant." In other words, Ruth was drawing a parallel to the comment Boaz made earlier about "finding shelter under the wings of God." Ruth was saying, *Boaz, would you become an instrument in God's protection of me? Would you do God's will by sheltering me? Can I find safety, shelter, love, and protection with you? Will you take me in?*

In that moment, Ruth was at her most vulnerable. She put all of her trust in Boaz's honor, and she was counting on Boaz not to take advantage of that vulnerability. Keep in mind what was going on during this scene at the threshing floor. Boaz – an older, unmarried man who had had a bit too much to drink – found himself with a beautiful, younger woman lying at his feet, making herself totally available to him, and promising to do whatever he wanted.

Guys… what would *you* have done?

Let's see what Boaz did:

(10) "The Lord bless you, my daughter," he replied. "This kindness is greater than that which you showed earlier: You have not run after the younger men, whether rich or poor. (11) And now, my daughter, don't be afraid. I will do for you all you ask. All my fellow townsmen know that you are a woman of noble character. (12) Although it is true that I am near of kin, there is a kinsman-redeemer nearer than I. (13) Stay here for the night, and in the morning if he wants to redeem, good; let him redeem. But if he is not willing, as surely as the Lord lives I will do it. Lie here until morning."
(14) So she lay at his feet until morning, but got up before anyone could be recognized; and he said, "Don't let it be known that a woman came to the threshing floor."
(15) He also said, "Bring me the shawl you are wearing and hold it out." When she did so, he poured into it six measures of barley and put it on her. Then he went back to town. (Ruth 3:10-15)

Is that not an amazing amount of self-control and restraint? Boaz was being honorable and protective. He not only protected Ruth from others, but he protected her from himself because, believe me, Boaz was having some thoughts there on the threshing floor. He honored Ruth by not taking advantage of her sexually. Boaz also honored the system and culture behind the concept of the kinsman-redeemer. He wanted to do it the right way: *Listen, Ruth. There is another man who is nearer to you, and we need to first give him the opportunity to become your kinsman-redeemer.* Boaz's actions on the threshing floor were consistent with the way he had lived his life up until that point: with honor and protectiveness.

(1) Meanwhile Boaz went up to the town gate and sat there. When the kinsman-redeemer he had mentioned came along, Boaz said, "Come over here, my friend, and sit down." So he went over and sat down.
(2) Boaz took ten of the elders of the town and said, "Sit here," and they did so. (3) Then he said to the kinsman-redeemer, "Naomi, who has come back from Moab, is selling the piece of land that belonged to our brother Elimelech. (4) I thought I should bring the matter to your attention and suggest that you buy it in the presence of these seated here and in the presence of the elders of my people. If you will redeem it, do so. But if you will not, tell me, so I will know. For no one has the right to do it except you, and I am next in line."
"I will redeem it," he said. (Ruth 4:1-4)

At this point in the story, some of us might be tempted to mock Boaz: *Way to go, Boaz! That's what you get for being so honorable. Nice guys never get the girl. You just lost Ruth to another dude because you had to do things the honorable way. You should have looked for a loophole or a shortcut. You blew it.*

Or did he?

(5) Then Boaz said, "On the day you buy the land from Naomi and from Ruth the Moabitess, you acquire the dead man's widow, in order to maintain the name of the dead with his property."
(6) At this, the kinsman-redeemer said, "Then I cannot redeem it because I might endanger my own estate. You redeem it yourself. I cannot do it." (Ruth 4:5-6)

There is no implication in the text that reveals why the kinsman-redeemer declined the offer after finding out about Ruth. Maybe he was already married? Maybe he didn't want to be connected to the Moabites? We don't know. But we *do* know that Boaz then became Ruth's kinsman-redeemer. So… does that mean if you make honorable decisions, then life will always turn out the way you want?

Absolutely not.

Sometimes, you can make the honorable decision, and you *won't* get the girl. Sometimes, you can make the honorable decision, and you *won't* keep your job. Sometimes, you can do the right thing, and you *won't* win the fight.

But… at the end of the day, you *will* keep your honor.

Do you have your honor? If so, what will it take to keep it? If not, what will it take to get it back? Who has God called you to protect? Are you being an instrument of God's protection to those people? Who do you claim to be important in your life, while your actions betray your words?

These are tough questions, I know. But this story of redemption isn't over yet.

Our true redeemer

Let me sum up the end of Naomi, Boaz, and Ruth's story. Boaz became Ruth's kinsman-redeemer, and the two were married. Then, Ruth – who had been barren her entire life – gave birth to a child. The attention of the story then turns back toward Naomi – the bitter, old woman who believed that God had turned his back against her:

(14) The women said to Naomi: "Praise be to the Lord, who this day has not left you without a kinsman-redeemer. May he become famous throughout Israel! (15) He will renew your life and sustain you in your old age. For your daughter-in-law, who loves you and who is better to you than seven sons, has given him birth."
(16) Then Naomi took the child, laid him in her lap and cared for him. (17) The women living there said, "Naomi has a son." And they named him Obed. He was the father of Jesse, the father of David. (Ruth 4:14-17)

Some significant information lies tucked in these verses. The baby, Obed, would one day become the father of Jesse. Jesse would eventually have eight sons, one of which would be a little shepherd boy named David… King David. Through a young woman, a bitter widow, and an honorable, protective man, God was doing something amazing. God was unveiling his plan. Naomi couldn't see that plan when her husband died in Moab. Naomi couldn't see that plan when her sons died. Naomi couldn't see that plan when she returned to Bethlehem a bitter, old woman. Ruth couldn't see that plan when she 'happened upon' a field owned by a man named Boaz. Boaz couldn't see that plan when he 'happened' to check on his field and find Ruth. Just like you and me, they were blinded by their circumstances, but God was doing something amazing.

God was paving the way for a king to be born. *King David?* Sure... but that's not the king I'm talking about.

The Gospel of Matthew begins with a genealogy. You know... one of those huge, boring family trees: *So-and-so begot so-and-so... who begot so-and-so... who begot so-and-so.* Genealogies are pretty easy to skip over, but right in the middle of this particular family tree, we learn some interesting information:

> **(5) Salmon the father of Boaz, whose mother was Rahab,**
> **Boaz the father of Obed, whose mother was Ruth, Obed the father of Jesse,**
> **(6) and Jesse the father of King David.**
> **David was the father of Solomon, whose mother had been Uriah's wife. (Matthew 1:5-6)**

If you were to continue reading, you would discover that this is the genealogy of Jesus. God was in the middle of Naomi's circumstances, and he was ushering in a plan of beautiful redemption. God was working through Boaz, the kinsman-redeemer, to ultimately redeem humankind through Jesus. God was at work in Bethlehem way before Mary and Joseph ever placed a baby in a manger.

God was ushering his son, Jesus, into our world, and no one would have ever predicted it or seen it coming. Did you notice the level of brokenness in that genealogy? Rahab: a prostitute. Boaz's wife, Ruth: a foreign widow. David: an adulterous murderer. The mother of David's son, Solomon, is only listed as someone else's wife: Uriah's wife. You think your family is jacked up? You've got nothing on Jesus' family. Through a prostitute, a widower, a murderer, and an adulterer – and that's just a few of the people on the list – God brought about the salvation of the world. Through a profound amount of brokenness, Jesus entered the picture.

The story of Ruth and Boaz is simply a foreshadowing of the greatest story ever told. Naomi and Ruth were distant, cut off, hopeless, and in need of a kinsman-redeemer. From Bethlehem, Boaz entered their lives. You and I are distant, cut off, hopeless, and in need of a redeemer. From Bethlehem, Jesus entered our lives. Boaz is merely an imperfect picture of Jesus. Jesus gathers distant, cut off, hopeless people like you and me under the shadow of his wings.

Jesus is our redeemer.

1. Matthew 23:37.

06. Boaz... Honor and Protectiveness
General Discussion Questions

Core:

1. How has your definition of manhood changed while reading *Grow A Pair*?

2. Naomi felt bitter toward God. Why did she feel this way, and have you ever found yourself in a similar frame of mind toward God?

3. Looking back at the struggles and circumstances you've survived throughout your life, have you been able to identify that God never abandoned you, but instead, had a plan for you?

4. Why was Boaz the type of man that other men looked up to?

5. How do you become an honorable man? How do you become a dishonorable man?

6. Do you have any areas of your life that are keeping you from regaining or furthering your honor?

7. In what direction are you headed? Are you headed toward honor or dishonor? Why?

8. *The diminishing return of sin always leads to the escalation of risk.* How do small compromises result in huge mistakes? In what ways have you experienced or witnessed the diminishing return of sin and the escalation of risk?

9. How does Boaz demonstrate protectiveness? How can *you* demonstrate protectiveness?

10. Sometimes doing the right and honorable thing won't work out the way you want, but you will keep your honor. Have you ever faced a situation in which you did the right thing, yet didn't experience the outcome you desired?

11. Are you protecting the most important parts of your life?

12. Do you still have your honor? If so, what will it take to keep your honor? If not, how will you reclaim your honor?

Challenge:

1. Take small steps toward maintaining or regaining your honor.

2. Reflect on God's definition of a true man, and ask him to help you grow into that definition.

06. Boaz... Honor and Protectiveness Discussion Questions for Women

Core:

1. How has your definition of manhood changed while reading *Grow A Pair*? Has your understanding of true manhood shaped your concept of what it means to be a godly woman?

2. When you think of an honorable, protective, male hero, who comes to mind?

3. In your experience, when have you felt most protected and honored?

4. Read Ruth 1. Based solely on this chapter, how would you describe Ruth's character?

5. Why do you think Ruth chose to stay with her mother-in-law?

6. Read Ruth 2. What does it mean to be an honorable man? Does honor look different for a woman? If so, how?

7. *The diminishing return of sin always leads to the escalation of risk.* What do you understand this phrase to mean? When have you experienced or witnessed the diminishing return of sin and the escalation of risk?

8. How does the diminishing return of sin lead you further away from being an honorable woman?

9. How would you compare and contrast Boaz's treatment of Ruth to David's response to his daughter's rape?

10. Read Psalm 36:7 and Psalm 57:1. What do these verses tell us about the nature of God's relationship with us?

11. In your own words, explain the concept of the *kinsman-redeemer*.

12. Compare the story of Ruth and Boaz with Jesus' arrival in this world as our redeemer.

13. Read Matthew 1:5-6. Do you recognize the names of the women in the family tree of Jesus who would have been considered women of 'questionable character'? What does this tell you about the nature of God?

Challenge:

1. Consider whether or not you are an honorable woman. What do you need to do to remain an honorable woman? What steps do you need to take in order to become more honorable?

2. As a woman, are there people in your life that you need to protect? Ask God to show you how to protect those people.

3. Reflect on God's definition of a true woman, and ask him to help you grow into that definition.

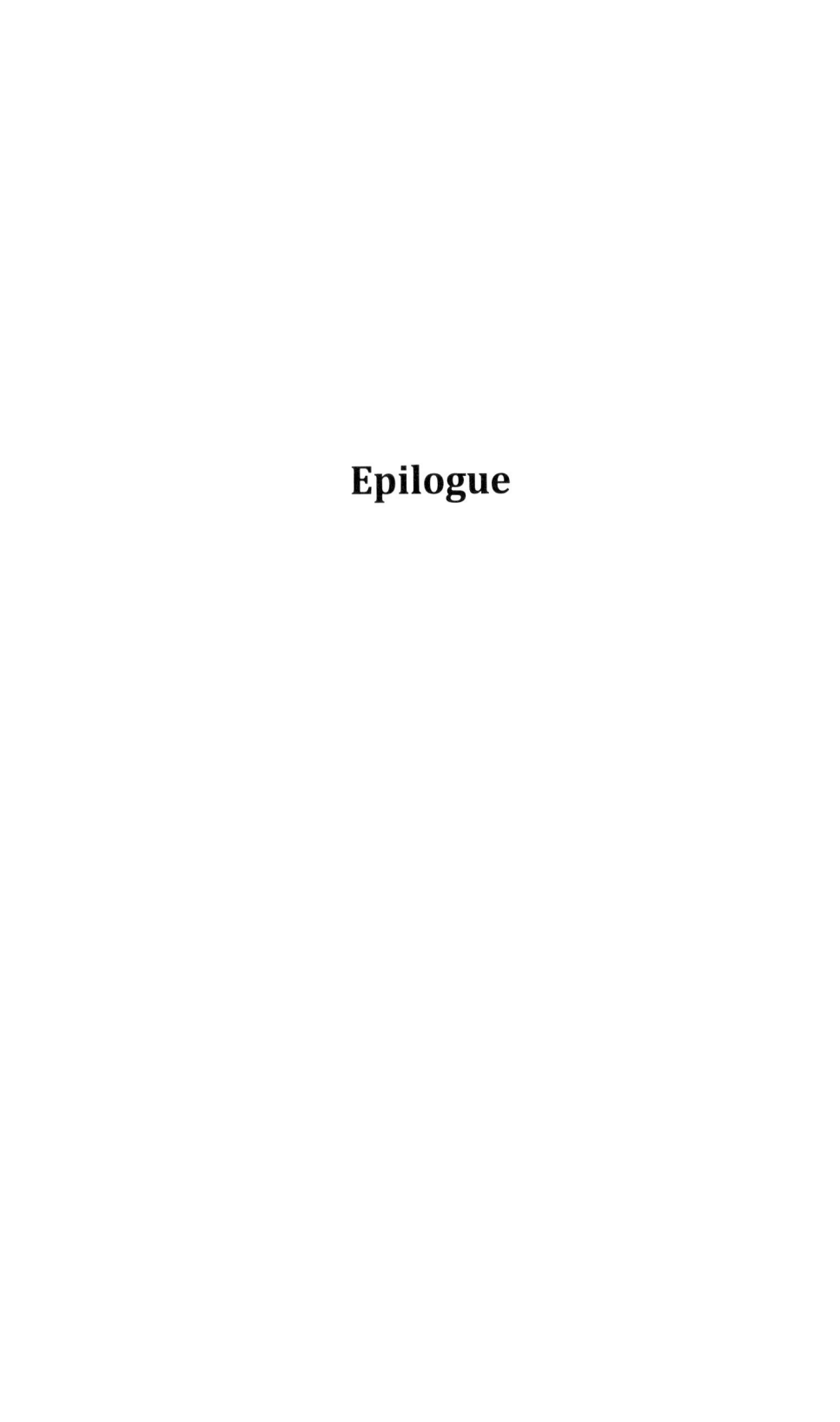

Epilogue

Epilogue

Throughout this book, we've presented some pretty heavy challenges, but here's the truth: with the exception of Jesus, no one has ever – or will ever – perfectly live up to these challenges. None of us can live perfect lives of identity, integrity, strength, wisdom, humility, honor, protectiveness, and a willingness to learn from our mistakes. We are all broken and flawed. Without Jesus, we are all disconnected from ourselves. We are all disconnected from one another. Most devastatingly, we are all disconnected from God.

But God has a plan. God has always had a plan. God sent us our ultimate redeemer in Jesus. Through Jesus, we are reconnected with our true identities, reconciled to one another, and redeemed into a relationship with God.

Jesus was and is the ultimate man. He was tempted in every way imaginable, but he withstood those temptations in order to display a life of perfection. He then placed the sins of the world on his back (which include every mistake and disaster you've ever been responsible for and ever *will be* responsible for) and nailed them to a cross. Through his death, our sins have been paid for. Through his resurrection, he offers us a better life.

Sure, the culmination of that better life is an eternity spent in heaven. But Jesus also offers a better alternative for the here and now. He doesn't want you to spend eternity in heaven after trudging through a miserable life on Earth (sounds a lot like Samson, doesn't it?). Instead, he wants you to spend eternity in heaven after enjoying a redeemed, altered, joyous life on Earth.

Becoming a person who knows their identity, lives it out with integrity, possesses a strength balanced by wisdom, responds to their sin with humility and a teachable attitude, and backs their honor up with protectiveness may sound like an impossible feat. When a godly lifestyle is written out like that, it does seem overbearing, doesn't it? But Jesus offers a better way. Jesus offers redemption. Jesus is looking at the relationships you've shattered and the appalling decisions you've made, and he is saying, *Follow me, and I'll lead you through this. Obey me, and I'll fix this. I know it sounds impossible, and change will definitely take some time, but through me, nothing is impossible.* Jesus offers grace, mercy, strength, and a changed life – both eternally and presently. All you have to do is follow him.

What does this mean? What does this look like in my life?

Men... this means you no longer have to look to your careers, your testosterone, or your physical abilities to find the definition of manhood. This means you no longer have to surrender your hopes, dreams, personalities, and masculinity at the doors of the church. This means you can finally work toward becoming the son, brother, friend, boyfriend, father, or husband that you've always deeply desired. This means you can find your identity in God rather than your strength, career, income, or sexuality.

Women... this means you no longer have to look to your careers, your sexuality, or your body image to find the definition of womanhood. This means you no longer have to surrender your hopes, dreams, personalities, and femininity at the hands of another man. Throughout this book, you've learned what a true, godly man – 'a man of standing' – looks like, and you don't have to settle for anything less. In fact, God commands that you *never* settle for anything less. A better life means you can finally become the daughter, sister, friend, girlfriend, mother, or wife that you've always deeply desired. This means you can find your identity in God rather than in media, pop culture, magazines, sexuality, or other men.

Doesn't this life sound better?

It is. And it's only a conversation away. Let Jesus into your life, follow and obey him, and watch in amazement as he beautifully redeems every aspect of your identity. Watch as he helps you gradually rely on and project the characteristics we've discussed in this book. Watch as you slowly transform into the man or woman you've always wanted to be, but never thought possible. Watch as Jesus makes your life better.

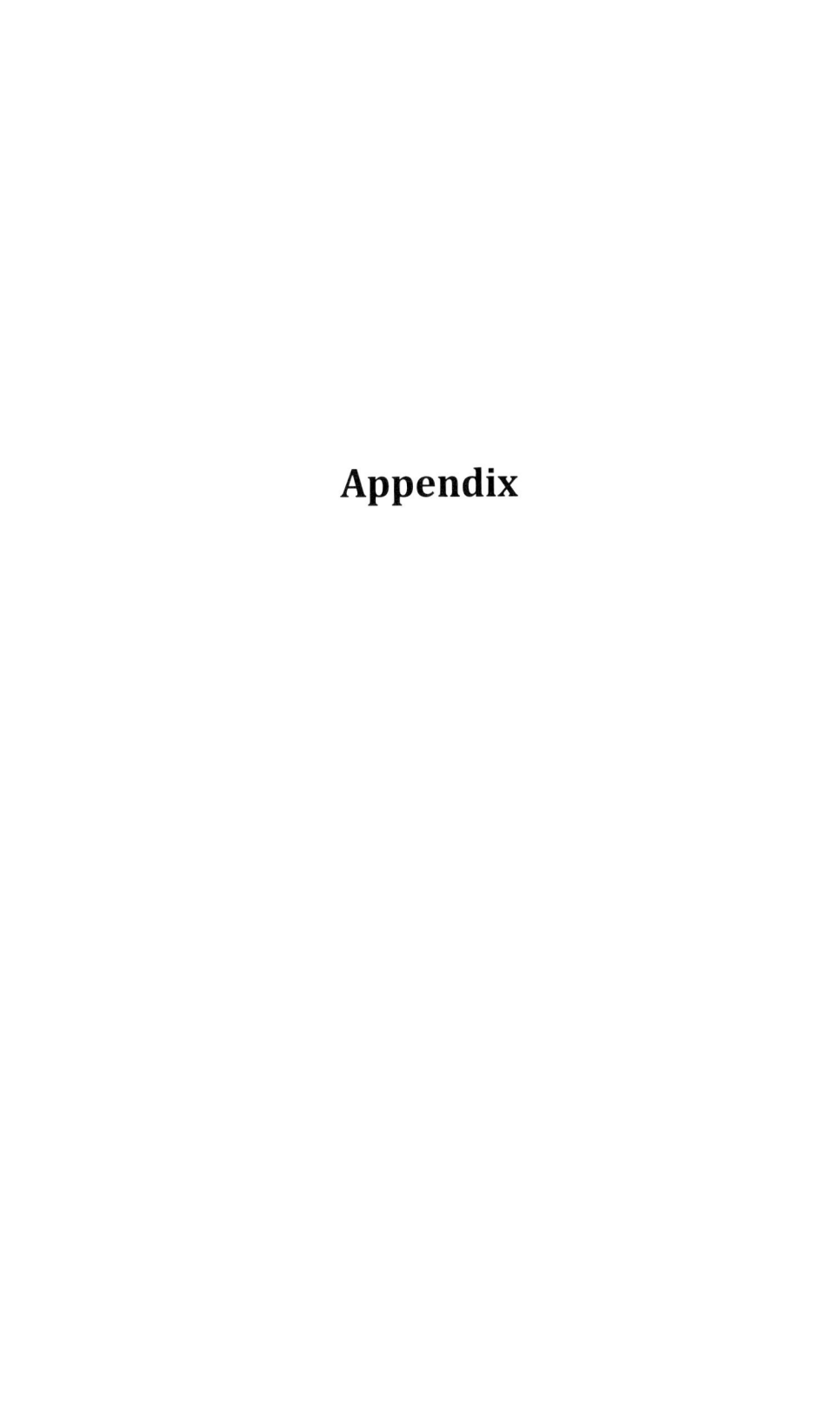

Appendix

Appendix

03. Samson and Vinnie... Strength and Wisdom

A note on marriage

In Judges 15:1-8, we see the ever-increasing carnage of Samson's decision to marry the wrong person, so let me take a minute to plead with those who are both married and unmarried. There are many marital lessons we can learn from Samson's life. Samson only wanted to marry the Philistine woman because of her physical beauty. When you are looking for someone to marry, you *must* look beyond that person's mere outward appearance. I don't mean that you should ignore outward appearance! Physical attraction plays a wonderful role in marriage, but beauty fades while character (whether good or bad) lasts a lifetime. I can't count the number of encounters I've had with men and women who have signed up for a life of pain and misery because they married someone without character.

Also, Samson probably had a 'visiting marriage' because he couldn't bring a Philistine wife home to his people. Therefore, his wife stayed at home with her father, and Samson would only visit when he wanted sex. He had no interest in providing for, living with, or loving his wife. He just wanted sex, and I wish I could say that this type of objective treatment is ancient history, but it's not. There are still men who have no interest in an actual relationship with their wives, yet they expect their wives to be sexually available whenever they want. This type of man is not a godly man. This type of man is not a *real* man.

05. David, Part Two... Learning From Mistakes

A note on parental discipline

I don't want to appear judgmental. I entirely understand why the concepts of *bad guilt* and *bad grace* are easy traps to fall into as parents. They are both born out of love for our children. However, these aren't the most loving responses we can have for our kids. In fact, God calls these reactions hateful:

> **He who spares the rod hates his son,**
> **but he who loves him is careful to discipline him. (Proverbs 13:24)**

Now, don't flip out. This verse has been twisted and misconstrued for a long time, but this verse does not call for abusive behavior. Instead, this verse is supposed to imply loving correction. Let me explain.

Shepherds carried a rod or staff in order to protect their sheep. The shepherd would nudge and prod the sheep to keep them on the right path and out of danger, and nowhere in the Bible do you find a shepherd beating his sheep. This verse is supposed to convey the following picture: *One day, a shepherd who took loving care of his sheep saw one of his flock walking toward a roaring river. The shepherd, who had nearly drowned in this same river before, knew the danger and quickly used his rod to pull the sheep back to safety. The shepherd used his staff to protect his sheep from the very river that had nearly killed him years ago.*

This verse implies that a good shepherd doesn't stand by and watch his sheep drown in the river. If you know how to protect your children, but you choose not to act on this knowledge, then you are concocting a hateful recipe for disaster.

Ironically, Solomon wrote this verse. Solomon, son of David and Bathsheba, watched his father's lack of initiative destroy his family. Solomon knew first hand that, when a father doesn't discipline his children, he hates them.

As a youth pastor, I consistently saw this same lack of initiative ruin kids' lives. I remember one specific conversation I had with a boy who was getting into trouble:

When is your curfew?

My parents don't care when I get home.

You drink a lot... what do your parents think about that?

My parents don't care if I drink. They buy it for me!

After a series of similar questions and answers, this kid froze mid-sentence and came to a terrible conclusion: *My parents don't care about me.* Then, we sat in silence together for a very long time.

God is a good father, and he disciplines his children out of love. If you are a parent, you are called to follow his perfect example.

About the Authors

Jim Burgen

Jim Burgen serves as Lead Pastor of Flatirons Community Church in Lafayette, Colorado. Jim also serves on the board of directors for SOZO International, a Non-Government Organization dedicated to bringing relief and development to war-torn communities in Central Asia. Jim attended Milligan College, receiving his degree in Bible and Sociology. Jim has authored several books, including those of the Flatirons Sermon Series Collection, and the Gold Medallion Award winner, *What's the Big Deal About Sex?* Jim lives with his wife, Robin, in Erie, Colorado.

Scott Nickell

Scott Nickell serves as Teaching Pastor of Flatirons Community Church in Lafayette, Colorado. Scott has passionately dedicated his life to helping people meet the authentic Jesus found in the Bible, rather than the commercialized version of Christ created by culture and (sometimes) the church. Scott attended Cincinnati Christian University, receiving his degree in Biblical Studies. Scott has authored the Flatirons Sermon Series Collection books. He lives with his wife, Alison, and his three children in Erie, Colorado.

Flatirons Sermon Series Collection

All My Life

Grow A Pair

PB&J: Key Ingredients for a Better Marriage